Dan Colchico

The Pride of Port Chicago

With
John Estes

Dan Colchico

The Pride of Port Chicago

With
John Estes

The San Francisco 49ers and the
Golden age of Football

San Francisco and the 49ers   1960 – 1967
New Orleans and the Saints   1968 – 1969

First Edition
June, 2012

Carroll Consulting Services

Copyright 2012 by John Estes

All rights reserved. No portion of this book may be reproduced, stored in a retrieval system or transmitted in any form or by any means – electronic, mechanical, photocopying – or otherwise without express written permission from Dan Colchico or John Estes.

All internal photographs are the property of the Dan Colchico Family Collection.

Cover photographs courtesy of Contra Costa County Historical Society,

Proofread by Nancy and Mindi Colchico
Proofread and Edited by Billie Reece
Proofread, Edited and Designed by Linda S. Kammeyer Schardt
Illustrations by: Joey Zubair
Cover design by C. John Estes
ISBN Number 978-1-4675-2183-3
Library of Congress Control Number: 2012911752

Printed in the United States by
Morris Publishing®
3212 East Highway 30
Kearney, NE 68847
1-800-650-7888
www.morrispublishing.com

How to order:

C. John Estes at: cje1enterprises@gmail.com
or by mailing your order and payment of $17.95+ $ 2.00 S/H + tax per book to:
        Carroll John Estes, C. C. S.
        5100-B1 Clayton Road #107
        Concord, CA 94521

This book has been inspired by my family and friends to let them know
how important they were in my life and in what I accomplished.

I didn't win them all, but I didn't quit either. I just kept going.

In Memory of my mother, Cecilia (Pat) Colchico

Acknowledgements

I owe a special thanks to those people listed below. They helped in the giving of their time and in relating common events that I hope made this work of words interesting and readable.

To my fellow teammates and opponents who after 50 years remembered me and gave credence to my play and friendship…

John Brodie	Lou Cordileone	Forrest Gregg
Paul Hornung	Billy Kilmer	Charlie Krueger
Howard Mudd	John Mellekas	Jim Otto
Ted Plumb	Len Rhode	Bob St. Clair
Y.A. Tittle	Abe Woodson	J. D. Smith
Charlie Krueger	R.C. Owens	*the late* Monty Stickles
Ben Scotti	*the late* John Gonzaga	*the late* Phil Parslow

To my great friends from "our" home town of Port Chicago and the surrounding towns in Contra Costa County… without all of you this journey might not have happened…

Dave Krowell	Larry Reece	Dennis Coffee
Marv McKean	Ollie McClay	Tommy Gott
Kilroy Johnson	Jim Bates	Curtis Easter
Russell Steele	Don Landrum	Charlie Zeno
Walt Jorgensén	Fatts DeMartini	Bino & Leo DeMarco
Conrad "Con" Stroer	Ralph McDonald	Kenny DeMartini
Mike Venn	Gizzy Galli	Bill Christ
Sam Papetti	Sil Garaventa	Guzzy Rizzo
Dave Beronio	Jerry Lombardi	Ralph McDonald
Mike Szymanski	Bob & Kay Massone	Slatz Mazzei
Al & Lynda Lorenzo	Paul Mendivil	Ronnie Johnson
Ray Mendioil	Stan Gaunt	Sam Arnold
Carlene Noran		

San Francisco's own Dick Boyd. *What a Ride!*

To all the others who came forward and added some little bits of local history that connected the dots of time over this 70 plus year journey.

Lou Aguilar	Joey Zubair	Jim Couchman
Gene Perry	Paul Thompson	

Contents

	PAGE #
INTRODUCTION	11
HERE'S DANNY	13
PORT CHICAGO "MY HOME TOWN"	15
HIGH SCHOOL	25
SAN JOSE STATE - 1957	36
1958-1959 AND A TOUCH FROM SAN FRANCISCO	43
SAN FRANCISCO- KEZAR	46
ROOKIE DAN COLCHICO 1960	49
THE CITY	63
SEASON 1961 THE LEAGUE SEASON EXPANDED TO 14 GAMES	67
1962 WINNING ON THE ROAD-LOSING AT HOME	72
1963 INJURIES- NOMELLINI AND ST. CLAIR RETIRE	75
1964 MY LAST HEALTHY SEASON	84
1965 THE INJURY	91
1966 FIGHTING FOR MY JOB	94
1967 MY YEAR OF COACHING	96
1968 THE BIG EASY	99
1969 THE END OF FOOTBALL	108
REMEMBRANCES	114
PLAYERS	115
BATTLEFIELDS	123

COACHES	125
OUR FIRST REUNION TO SAY GOODBYE-A LITTLE POEM THAT MADE US CRY	134
GOLF MORE GOLF AND SAVING ST.CLAIR	137
RAGE IN THE NFL	141
MORE MUSING'S	146
THE "ME" "ME" "ME" NFL	148
TEAM MATES AND FRIENDS	157
LIFE AFTER FOOTBALL	164
PHEWING IN ALASKA	164
BACK TO FOOTBALL FOR A GOOD CAUSE	173
WRAPPING IT UP	175
THE COLCHICO TEAM	176
FINAL…FINAL…FINAL	177

Introduction

How does one describe a man like Dan Colchico? Bigger than life? One of a kind? Over the top? A one hundred and ten per- center? Well, he is all of these and more. You could also add gruff and rugged to the list.

Ted Plumb is a fellow Mt. Diablo classmate class of 1957 who, in his professional career, played for the Minnesota Viking's and was an assistant coach and personal manager in the NFL for 30 years. Ted coached the Super Bowl Champions 1985 Chicago Bears and the Super Bowl Champions 1999 Saint Louis Rams. He stated "Dan was one of the most physical football players I ever saw."

Bob St. Clair, NFL Hall of Fame inductee and 49er teammate comments "I credit much of my success to Dan Colchico, who played so aggressively against me on each and every down during practice that by the time I played against my opponent on Sunday, I felt like I had gotten a break."

But Dan is also a very kind, generous, gentle and loving person. I saw this first-hand one evening as I walked into his trophy and memorabilia-filled garage where he conducts his business. There he was Grandpa Dan sitting down trying to teach one of many young granddaughters the Julius La Rosa song "Eh Cumpari" - forefinger and thumb pinched together while keeping time with the rhythm, singing each word and note to his obviously delighted student.

If he likes you he will do anything for you. If he doesn't, well, there would be no reason for you to come around.

I grew up in Concord in the 50's and 60's in the Mt. Diablo class of 1963. I saw Dan play in the old Kezar Stadium. He spoke at our Winter High School Sports banquet in 1962. I had also met Dan a few times over the years; a big man with a deep voice and big hands.

As time passed and as the 49ers became one of the preeminent NFL teams in the 80's and 90's, Dan's persona began to take on a local legendary status. He had played on some of the greatest Mt. Diablo

High School football teams from the past, was a two-time All-American from San Jose State, a 49er Eshmont award winner, a defender of Port Chicago, Alaskan Salmon fisherman, car and beer salesman and a local liquor store owner.

So what made this person of interest someone to write about? We will start at the beginning. 75 years ago and follow the life of the "The Pride of Port Chicago, in a straight forward, no holds barred story of a man who lived his life the way he wanted to and who played against and with some of the greatest players of all time in what some have called the "Golden Age of Professional Football"; his story told by him and others who knew him.

John Estes

Here's Danny

On Monday, May 27, 1937 in Berkeley, California, Daniel Mametta Colchico came roaring into this world, the only child of Joseph Mario and Cecelia Colchico (maiden name "Palubicki"). Joseph, a champion swimmer in Milan, Italy, immigrated to the United States from Verano Borghi Lombardi, Italy in 1920 by way of St. Johns, New Brunswick. Then down to Boston he came as Mario Giuseppe Colchico, his birth name. Shortly after his arrival into the United States, Mario Giuseppe changed his name to Joseph Mario because he wanted to be an American so bad, according to Dan, "He just wanted to be called Joe. "Hey 'Joe."

Joe, as most immigrants in the early 20th Century, was sponsored by one of the prominent local Contra Costa families, the Vasconis. Antonio Vasconi was the patriarch of this influential household and had a tremendous appreciation for the opportunities that this nation afforded its citizens. Cecelia with her parents along with two of her sisters migrated to California from Minnesota. The Palubicki family would grow to nine children over the next few years. Joe and Cecelia met while working at General Chemical in Nichols, Ca. They married in 1929 and settled in Berkeley., "My dad could not speak much English and my mother, being from Polish immigrant parents, wasn't much better - but it all worked out."

Two years after Dan's birth, Joe and Cecelia, packed up and moved to the other side of the East Bay hills and set up housekeeping in a little town called Port Chicago, where Cecelia had been raised as a child.

Cecelia Susan Colchico and Dan – just starting in 1937

...and proud Papa Joe holding a future "49er".

Port Chicago "My Home Town!"

The area that became Port Chicago was where Dan attended grade school and then walked to Concord to attend high school. Dan made life-long friends and this was the community that would forever shape the character of this man. "My home town," he would say, is a low lying piece of land sitting on the shores of the Suisun Bay, mostly marching towards the north bay and gently rolling hills protecting the south side, approximately 1 to 1-1/2 miles from the shore.

The first inhabitants to this region were the "hunter gatherer" Chupcan Bay Miwok Indians, who plied the shallow streams and bay inlets for food and shelter. The Spanish first explored this area in the 1770's with the first Spanish settlers arriving in the 1820's. During the early 20th century, Italian and Portuguese hunters and fishermen, mostly from Martinez to the west and Pittsburg and Antioch to the east, worked this abundant ground for their livelihoods and a few settled here.

Port Chicago was first called Bay Point, but in 1931 Walter Van Winkle, a prominent business leader at the time, was able to get the town name changed to Port Chicago, and the Port Chicago Post Office ran from 1931 to 1969.

This is the town Dan moved to with his mom and dad in 1939; quiet, unincorporated with a population of maybe 1200. He attended Bay Point Elementary in Port Chicago where he met some of the local kids that would play an important part in his early growing years and remain lifelong friends, Dave Krowell, Kilroy Johnson, Mo Estes, Jim Powell, Reno Piva, Bob Malloy, Ollie McClay, Curtis Easter, Jim Bates, Larry Reece, and Roy Johnson. They all played a very important part in Dan's life. We won't say what color they are. Would it change the story? Does it really make any difference? No, it does not.

Dan stated about his friends, "We would be out all day doing something. We were never home. The boys from Clyde, Lefty Butler and Burly Biles, and the kid from Nichols, Benny Venturino, came around a lot. We were like brothers. While attending elementary school, I, along with Curtis Easter, Jim Bates and others, won the Bay Point Class A Basketball Championship in the spring of 1951."

College, the 49ers and the NFL opened up new worlds to Dan back then. Port Chicago was like the "melting pot of America." It was a rugged town with different types of ethnic and racial groups. They were generally all poor in a financial way but that made them work hard and support each other so they could all get ahead. The bonds built between friends and neighbors to this day remain mostly unbreakable. They are still helping each other. A man was only as good as his word. You shook hands and the deal was done. If someone broke the code, everyone in town knew. That type of loyalty from the individuals who live on your street, who live in your community, is what makes a place a Home Town.

This quiet little town would change forever as it would leap into the 20th Century shortly after the Japanese attack on Pearl Harbor, Hawaii, on December 7, 1941. The Navy claimed part of this area that same month, and began building the Port Chicago Naval Magazine, now known as the Concord Naval Weapons Station. Dan would remain in Port Chicago until he was literally forced off his property. US Marshalls came and served him eviction papers some 28 years later during the height of the Vietnam War. Dan, not giving up, would fight the United States Navy, the Federal Government, and the State of California over the next few years in an attempt to save his home and his beloved town of Port Chicago from destruction.

Tragedy struck early in Dan's life as his father Joe was killed on the job in December of 1943. Dan was six and a half years old. "My mother was handed a check for $19.50, not even $20.00! What can you say? I still have that check. My mother worked all her life. She took the bus, rode in carpools; she even hitch-hiked when necessary. She never learned how to drive and she never missed a day of work. She did the best she could."

"I remember my Dad very well, as well as a six year-old can. Everyone in those days had a garden in the front, side or back yard, wherever you could grow something. On the weekends, he and I would drive into Pittsburg, then over Kirker Pass, all the way out to Clayton Road and into Walnut Creek. In those days it was all walnut and almond orchards. We carried every type of vegetable from swiss chard, tomatoes and beans, my father would sell and trade with other farmers along the way. We were struggling to make ends meet like everyone else, but we ate well. Those were great days for me, as I remember.

"My dad was maybe 5'9" but he never backed down from anything. He was so proud to be in America - to be an American - that he did not teach me how to speak Italian. Some say that was wrong but that was the way he wanted me to live the American dream. My father arrived in this country in 1920. Immigration laws were very different back then. First, if you didn't pass the medical examination you were sent back to whatever country you came from, and if you did not have a job waiting for you or if you did not have a sponsor, you could also be sent back to your home country."

What most don't know about that time in our nation is that the sponsoring individual or individuals of a newly arriving immigrant were responsible, for a time of one year, to find that new person a job. The sponsor could also be held liable for any debts or penalties that may have been accumulated by that person over that one-year probation period. So you can see what the immigrant was expected to do that was coming to the United States during the beginning years of the last century; that being to assimilate, to step up to the plate, get a job and move this country forward. "My father even went to night school to learn about America... to learn its laws, its customs, its form of free enterprise," Dan said. "He received his Diploma in Naturalization from Alameda Evening High School on June 12, 1935, one of the happiest days of his life. It took 15 years to get that diploma because during the day, he was working to pay back those who had faith in him and to save some money for a future family. Unlike today when so many come to this country illegitimately and do not flow into the American mainstream, but simply live off the labor of others. My father was not an Italian-American; he was an American who happened to be born Italian.

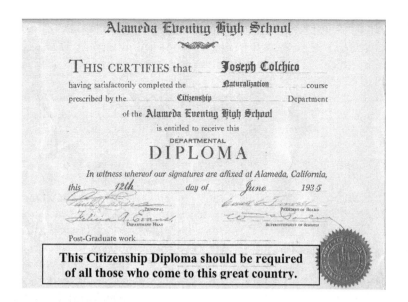

Grandpa Palubicki and me - 1938

"When he died, it threw our family into some turmoil so my Grandfather Leo Palubicki, Grandma Palubicki, my mother's father and mother, along with my uncles Ernie and Andy Palubicki, began to take over some of the duties of rearing a young boy with great energy.

"My Grandfather Leo lost a leg to diabetes before I could remember and he walked using crutches. He was as strong as an ox. Two or three times a month we would walk a mile or so out of town in the direction of Martinez to our favorite fishing spot near Swanton's - a little fishing store and eatery just off frontage road on the bank of one of the many inlets from the bay. He never complained. We would filet the fish where we caught them and bring them home for dinner. He was comfortable with who he was and what he looked like. When you approached him he would puff out his chest and greet you with a smile and a strong hand shake. I played cribbage with him every day in his room. When he lost his other leg to the same disease, he never said a word about it. When you came into his room he would pull himself upright, puff out his chest and give you that smile. I lost him when I was nine. He taught me not to be afraid of who I am; I miss him to this day.

"Swanton's made the best damn hamburgers anywhere. On weekends during the summer you would find cars parked all along the road. People would be standing outside having a beer and a burger, just enjoying the day. Then the powers that be blocked off the road and a little piece off Contra Costa history disappeared.

"My uncles had two distinctly different personalities. Both were graduates of Mt. Diablo, Andy was more open and more at ease with people. Ernie was more withdrawn. Ernie, nick-named 'Gump,' had been a tremendous athlete in high school in the late 20's. When he graduated in 1930, he received offers to college and many thought he had professional potential. But in those days the family came first and he was told he had to stay and support the family. I feel he held a lot of resentment inside because he really wanted to do all that he felt his talent could bring him. He was also the disciplinarian in the family. When he told me to go into the shed and wait for him because of some incident I did that everyone thought was bad enough to be punished for, I knew he was going for the strap. But the worst part of it all was that he would let me sit there for hours and that would drive me crazy. I just wanted the beating so I could get back outside and do other things. I think he got some kind of perverse pleasure out of doing this.

"Uncle Andy on the other hand taught me how to work on cars. We could tear cars apart and put them back together again for hours. He was stern but not hard. They were both good men. From Ernie I learned intensity - from Andy, to live a little but always complete the job.

Uncle Ernie (Gump) Palubicki and Dan – 1947.

Uncle Andy Palubicki, United States Navy, 1946.

"There was also my Uncle Roy Mattson, who had married my mother's sister Pauline, and one of his sons, Donny, who was like the bother I never had. Roy was somewhat of a father figure and helped bring some stability to our ever-changing world. When we were young, Roy would take us to fun places. He was head of the carpenters' union and when we were teens he often made it possible for us to get jobs. In high school, Donny and I played football together.

"Across the street from my house was Cotton Brown's garage. Cotton was quite a character and he was the best mechanic around. The 1950's and early 1960's were the heyday of Hot-Rod shows; people from all over brought their Hot-Rods and Show Cars to Cotton to be worked on. Cotton's was one of the places we would hang out from time to time.

"The DeMarco brothers, Leo and Bino - they were both older than I and great Mt. Diablo athletes. Leo played football, basketball and baseball through the war years, the early 40's, while Bino played varsity baseball for 4 years in the late 40's.

"Americo "Firpo" Grossi was one of the greatest athletes in Mt. Diablo High School history during the mid 30's. He once put a 16 pound shot over 50 feet in high school. When he shook your hand you knew you had met a man. The Grossi's were a wonderful family. Firpo's son Dave went on to play football for Stanford. These men, along with Johnny Gonzaga and John Henry Johnson, were my sports heroes.

"We were all home the night of July 17, 1944 when the ammunition ship exploded at the loading dock on the base. We were far enough away that we had little damage done to our house. My mother worked in the pay-masters office on the base and for weeks after the explosion she worked day and night sending out relief checks to those injured and to families of those who were killed. My grandmother, who lived with my Uncle Ernie four houses down the street, lost an eye during the explosion due to flying glass. This was one of the biggest injuries in the town.

"Loyalty was the key word in my family. The family came first. You took care of the needs at home, as it was with my Uncle Ernie. He didn't like being kept back from the things he wanted to do but he stayed home; in those days a family had to stick together or you didn't eat.

"As I began to grow and make friends in school that word 'loyalty' would become the most important part of any bond I had with any of my friends. We were from Port Chicago, 'The wrong side of the tracks.' We had to stick together. When not in school or out doing something else, we hung at each other's houses, at the pool hall or at Cotton's Garage. I'm proud to say that most of these friendships remain strong to this day."

Pool Hall – Port Chicago – Christmas, 1951

"A quick side note. Years later, Pop sold the pool hall to Ralph Jacobsen. Ralph was an easy touch and gave credit to just about everyone. When the Navy tore the town down, he lost some money. I paid him the $45 I owed. The guys above did also.

"Bay Point Elementary had kids coming from Port Chicago and other rural parts in the area. I remember Marlon Lyson and Johnny Garcia. Johnny and I became fast friends and we started collecting other kids in town - Kilroy Johnson, Dave Krowell, Jim Bates, Larry Reece, Curtis Easter, Reno Piva (a great high school pole vaulter), Tommy Gott, Paul Mendivil, Paul Lang, Sam Arnold; all these guys became the core of our sports teams. Some called us a gang. We didn't care – we were friends. As we got older, very few from 'outside' wanted to mess with us. Unlike today's kids, we stuck together and helped move each other forward. I was one of the speakers at Tommy's 25th Anniversary dinner honoring him for outstanding service at Allied Chemical. We were all happy when one of us became successful. When I began to make it in football, they all gave me support which helped a lot during some rough times. No one tried to pull you back to the streets. It was as if when one of us did something good - took a step forward to success - we all went with that person. That's quite a feeling and that's why, when I could, I brought them with me to dinners, banquets, got them sideline passes, into some team parties - anything that made us feel we all had accomplished something together.

"Any vacant lot became our playing field. We played football and we even got our own sand and made base pads for baseball games. It was in one of these fields when we were playing some game that Bob Mallory got his unfortunate nickname. There was a weed chopper clearing one side of the field and for some reason neither the driver of the chopper or Bob noticed each other. Bob was going for the ball when he was run over by the chopper cutting off his fingers on both hands thus the handle 'Stubs.' Bob didn't let it stop him. He turned out to be one hell of a second baseman, and even made a career for himself as a barber. We all had a basketball rim, very few with netting, nailed to any barn or garage if you had one. We could play games around the clock. I didn't get home until my mother's curfew which was ten o'clock almost every night. I would drink a quart of milk, eat three or four sandwiches and go to bed. I never got fat; we were all too active, outside doing something. In the mid 40's and early 50's most of us didn't have a TV. If someone did, it was black and white and small. We didn't sit around all day eating chips, drinking Coke and getting lazy; we were outside getting sun and staying healthy.

"We knew where all the fruit trees were, and when they were in season we would eat ourselves sick. Sometimes the trees were in someone's backyard; we could jump the fence real fast and run like hell if we had to, but most knew us and it was okay. Like I said, we were a rough bunch of guys but we never destroyed property on purpose; we respected our elders. My friends would even come over and help clean my mother's home, and I did likewise. My mother was the boss - period! You feared your parents more than anyone else and that's how it should be.

"During the summer and after school, if we weren't playing a game, we would go fishing or hunting, carrying a .22 rifle around town in those days, which even as a boy of ten or eleven didn't panic anyone. We knew the rules and if someone did something wrong, everyone in town knew about it. The shame it brought was enough to keep us in line. There were times though that a few of us crossed the line, but more on that later.

"Everyone was trying to make a buck, jobs were few and the pay, well let's say was just enough to get some food and keep a roof over our heads and not much left over. My mother worked twelve to fourteen hour days sometimes, six days a week. She worked all her life and I never heard her complain. She would say be thankful you have a job.

"One of the businesses in town that helped support a large growing population of young boys and girls was the Port Chicago Theatre owned by Joe Myers. He employed most of us at one time or another during our elementary and early high school years.

Saturday Matinee – Christmas Circa 1948 – 1950
Can you find yourself?

"I had a paper route at nine, ran errands for the local store owners, traded in beer and Coke bottles if I found them before my buddies did; it was all fair game. As I got older I picked fruit in Brentwood and shot a little pool and a few other things. Most of it went to the house. I always had some coins in my pocket; 50 cents went a long way back then.

"I pretty much came and went as I wanted to. I tried not to upset my mom too much but I'm sure I did at times. I would go hunting and wouldn't come home until 2 or 3 in the morning. I would go into the kitchen and cook up some pasta and I would hear my mom calling out 'that sure smells good,' so, of course, I would take her some. She was strong; she had to be to put up with me. When she got mad at me, which was often, and she wanted to make a point, she'd poke her index finger into my chest so hard I still have a dent in my upper chest to this day. Well, that's what I tell people anyway.

"When we were forced out of our homes in Port Chicago in 1969, we moved to Concord. Nancy and I had a spare room off our garage and we turned it into her living area. I told her, now, mom, you are the grandma, you do not have to discipline any of my kids running around here. You tell me what may have happened and I will be the disciplinarian. Well, her grand kids did pretty much what they wanted to do; they ran all over the place; they would even jump off the garage roof into the pool. You know, she never snitched on them once. I think she thought, 'These kids are a breeze. I'll let Dan take care of his own problems. I'm taking a break.'"

High School

"I was a tall, lanky kid when I entered Mt. Diablo High my freshman year in 1951. I was kind of a rough kid. Some of the teachers and coaches thought I was a little out of hand at times - for one thing they didn't like my DA hair cut - short for Ducks Ass. I thought 'the hell with them.' I wasn't going to cut it. I was often rebellious - maybe sometimes to a fault but that's who I was and who I am today.

"I made the freshmen football team and later in the season I was moved up to the JV team. We all had a locker in the gym where we would hang our uniforms and we put all types of other things in there. One day I came to practice and someone had stolen my money out of my locker! That did it - I chose to call the whole team out. I was going to whip everyone on the team until someone told me who took the money. Well, the coach found out about what I had said and he wanted me to go and apologize to the team. I told him I was not going to do it unless I got my money back. I will not apologize to anyone. I didn't play any football the rest of that year."

Along with Russell Steele, another Mt. Diablo great athlete, Dan made the JV Baseball team in the spring of 1952. He could hit for power if not for average and was quite an imposing figure at first base.

That fall the football season of 1952 saw Dan, now a sophomore, move into the varsity and his first undefeated 7 wins, 1 tie and championship team. That team produced the leading ball carrier in Northern California. That season Bill Edleman rushed for over 1200 yards, earning him High School All-American honors. Bill received scholarship offers from all over the country. He opted to stay home and work in his father's business. Dan states, "He would have been great any place he went." The two men who coached this team would change the way Mt. Diablo played football and turn them into winners. Rod Franz would lead Mt. Diablo to the championship this year and next with his assistant coach John Ralston.

John Ralston – 1952
Varsity Baseball Coach

John Ralston played linebacker for the University of California playing in two Rose Bowls before earning his degree in 1951. Leaving Diablo after the 1953 baseball season, Ralston would continue to build a long and illustrious coaching career. Starting at San Lorenzo High then onto Utah State in 1959 before taking job at Stanford in 1963. John would build a 55 win, 36 loss and 3 tie record over nine seasons. He also won back-to-back PAC 8 Championships in 1970 and 1971, and with Heisman Trophy winning quarterback Jim Plunkett, defeated Ohio State and Michigan in the Rose Bowl those same years. He would coach the Denver Broncos from 1972 to 1976 and become an assistant coach for the San Francisco 49ers, Philadelphia Eagles, and the Toronto Argonauts in the Canadian Football League. Head coach for the Oakland Invaders in the short lived United States Football League from 1983 to midterm 1984. John even coached the Dutch Lions, the National Football Team for The Netherlands winning the Bronze in the European Championships in Helsinki Finland in 1991. John Ralston was inducted into the Mt. Diablo High School Sports Hall of Fame in 2005.

After football in 1951, Dan went out for the basketball team and was doing pretty well until, "I got caught smoking behind the coaches house and was cut from the team; so what do I do? I go and get a bunch of my hometown buddies. We formed a team of our own and beat both the JV team and the varsity. We even played John Swett and beat them. Now that's pay back. As I moved through the rest of my high school years, I learned to understand the reasons behind these coaches' decisions. The best thing though was that we won."

The 1953 baseball season saw Dan move up and down between the JV and Varsity teams lettering on the Varsity team with a season record of 10 wins and 7 losses.

Dan started his junior year as the starting offense and defense end on what would become the legendary Mt. Diablo Sports Hall of Fame undefeated football team with 8 wins 0 losses in 1953. They were coached by the also legendary, three-time All-American guard from The University of California, Rod Franz.

In the three seasons Franz coached at Mt. Diablo, he compiled a record of 21 wins, 2 losses and 1 tie, going 6 and 2 in 1951 for second place in the League; winning 7 and tying 1 for the League co-championship in 1952; winning 8, losing none for the undisputed championship in 1953. Mt. Diablo was the last high school team he would coach.

Coach Franz
Varsity Football –

He was inducted into The College Football Hall of Fame in 1977 and to the Mt. Diablo High School Sports Hall of Fame in 2007.

It was during the season of 1953 that Cliff Mores wrote his Concord Transcript column "The Scoreboard" and called Dan a "rugged, roaring flank defender, may turn out to be the best defensive wingman in the CCCAL." Forty-one years later in 1994, in a poll conducted by the Contra Costa Times after interviewing 68 coaches, sports writers, teachers and local historians, they selected the All-Time Contra Costa County Football Team; Dan made the first team on the defensive line.

1953 Football Team

First Row, Left to Right –
Walter Dobbs (Mgr), Jim Serventi (Mgr), Marlon Henvit (Co. Cap.), Russ Steele (Co. Cap), Bob Gotshall (Mgr)

Second Row:
Carol Halverson, Aurelia Omania, Jerry Sisson, Jack Robbins, Jim Bates, Walt Titcomb, Jerry Taylor, Tom Ready, Jack Jones, Phil Parslow, Larry Reece, Al Boot, John Wingfield, Bill Rood, Laura Sheley, Sandra Chrisensen.

Third Row:
Marlene Adams, Dan Larscheid, Jerre DeRosa, Hart Fairclough (Coach), Bud Torres, Shelbe Higgins, John Davis,
Stan Gaunt, Jim Kelly, John Williams, Dick Gierak, Roger Mills, Dave Woklgemuth, Jim Walsh, Paul Buckman, Harold Hayworth, Rod Franz (Coach), Billie Trimble, Liz Lucero

Fourth Row:
Sid Simmons, Dan Colchico, Don Mattson, Harry Haley, Robbie Himsl, Freddy Crabaugh, Marv McKean, Louis Fridrich, Ed McGill, Jim Davis, Bill Leuth, Ed Ruiz, Frank Gonzaga.

The 1953 team produced other fine football players. Russell Steele class of 1954 would go on to play for Chuck Taylor at Stanford on varsity seasons 1955-1957. Stan Gaunt "Full-Back" class of 1954 would gain 872 yards for a 8.5 yard per carry average that season and go on to East Contra Costa College. Stan was also the CIF State pole vault champion that spring of 1954. Marv McKean class of 1954 and starting quarterback on both undefeated 1952 and 1953 teams would play at East Contra Costa College, then went on to San Jose State where Dan would join him in 1957. Phil Parslow of class of 1954 Honorable Mention All-League End that year would go on to be a starting halfback for U.C.L.A and later to play for the Baltimore Colts and San Diego Chargers in the early 1960's. Phil went on after his playing days to be a very successful Hollywood Director and Producer working for Disney Studios and on such 1980's TV shows asFalcon Crest and Dynasty.

The Mt. Diablo High School Sports Hall of Fame inducted Russell Steele in 2005, Stan Gaunt in 2003, and Marv McKean in 2004.

The following spring of 1954 saw Dan come into his own as a baseball player. The varsity team, led by Don Landrum and coached by Willard "Bill" Knibbe, went 13 and 3 for the season and placed second in the League. Dan batted .280 and played a fine first base. In one memorable game on May 6th in Antioch, with Antioch leading 6 to 0 in the fifth inning, one of the Antioch players spiked Dan on first base - that's when the fight started. Coach Knibbe pulled his team from the field and filed a protest. Antioch was later awarded a forfeit win. "He got me good but I got him better," said Dan.

Dan – Mt. Diablo 1st Baseman

Teammate Landrum class of 1954 and one of Diablo's finest athletes, he lettered in basketball, baseball and track, making All-League in both baseball and basketball. He then went on to play professional baseball for the Philadelphia Phillies, St. Louis Cardinals, Chicago Cubs and retired with the San Francisco Giants in 1966. Don was inducted into The Mt. Diablo Sports Hall of Fame in 2003.

Don's father always wanted him to be a professional baseball player and wouldn't allow him to play football in high school.

Who knows how great he could have been. Don, battling cancer, passed away in 2003 only a few months before he was inducted into the Mt. Diablo Hall of Fame.

A new head coach took over the Varsity football team for the 1954 season, Orval Steffen. He would be assisted by a future Mt. Diablo Hall of Fame inductee, Hart Fairclough. Senior Co-Captain Colchico led his team to a 4 win, 3 loss, 1 tie season and third place in the League. Dan would be named on the All-DVAL football first team and second team All-Northern California. His bruising, all-out-battering-ram style of play would be Dan's trademark for the remainder of his career. But following this successful season, Dan jumped right into the beginning of the rest of his life.

"Football was over, and with little to do until baseball next spring, I thought, 'I'll ask my girlfriend, Nancy, if she wants to get married.'

Nancy and I had been going together five months. I had a few bucks in my pocket so in late November I popped the question, and I'll be damned, she said, 'Yes.' I told her I had won some money at the hard top races in Pacheco so we were headed to Reno. The first thing I did was fill up the gas tank, picked up my buddy Dave Krowell and we were off. States Nancy, 'He probably won the money at the pool hall. That's where he spent a lot of his time.' I really didn't care. I was off on an adventure for the rest of my life. When we got to Reno it was Saturday afternoon. We bought the license at the courthouse; then found a Catholic Church. We asked them if they would marry us. Well they damned- near laughed us out of town so we went back to the courthouse. We had Dave and the building janitor stand up for us and we both said, 'Yes, I do.' We drove back to town late that night. I dropped Nancy off at her place and I went home to mine. No one but a select few knew. We didn't tell our parents until after June graduation. Nancy was 16. I was 17."

Dan was named captain of the varsity baseball team the spring of 1955, and between games he participated in track and field events taking fourth place in the County Championship Track Meet in the shot put. Next, college was coming, along with responsibility.

"A footnote on my high school experience... There were a number of persons back then that had a great deal of impact on my life. Some helped me to become street wise, while others helped get me through high school. I had a car and pretty much drove to school every day during my senior year. I started driving when I was 13 but I didn't have a car then so I walked or hitch-hiked most everywhere I went.

"One of my early in life mentors was a great man, Pete Kramer. He was the Dean of Boys when I was there, but had been a coach and teacher at Mt. Diablo from 1925 to 1949. As you may have figured out by now, I was not a real good student. I missed a lot of school. I had a pile of absentee forms always signed by my mother with numerous excuses as to why I could not be at school on a certain date: My uncle had died; an aunt or a distant cousin had passed away. Well, one day in my senior year, Mr. Kramer came over to me outside of class, put his arm around my shoulders and said, 'Dan, since you have killed off three-quarters of your family, I think the rest would like to hang around awhile so I can expect to see more of you at school.'

"I did finish out that year and I did spend a few more hours in the halls of education. Pete Kramer was a man of honesty and integrity. To this day my signature still looks a lot like my mom's.

"Miss Lum was a woman of tremendous self-discipline and patience. She was a teacher, a mentor; someone that any student at any time could come to for teenage advice. She was the head of the school newspaper and I was the sports editor. And let me tell you, it took all the patience she had to control and try to refine someone as rough as I was. But like every other kid in school I got the feeling she really cared for us, that she wanted to see all of us move forward in life. She was the boss; I knew it and I respect her to this day. Both have passed on.

"One other man I owe a great debt to is Coach Rod Franz. If he had not talked to me and worked with me when I got back on the football team, I have no idea in what direction I would have gone. All I can say is everything worked out fine, Coach."

Dan was inducted as a charter member into the Mt. Diablo High School Sports Hall of Fame in 2003.

Nancy and me – Sr. Prom, 1955

"My father was the first to find out about Dan and I being married," states Nancy. "He found a letter from Dan calling me, 'my darling wife.' Dad wasn't too happy about it but he never really got mad either. According to Dan, when he told his mom about us right after school was out, the first thing she said was, 'You're too young. I'll have the marriage annulled. Where would you live? It won't work.' 'But, mom, Nancy's pregnant' Dan stated. Everything changed right then. 'We have to find a priest. You must get married in church. I'll arrange everything,' said his mother. Dan's mother and I became very close right from the start.

She was always good to me and was never one of those meddling mothers-in-law. I took the required Catholic pre-marriage training classes, and in September, at this time I was over six months pregnant, Dan and I were married again, this time in a Catholic Church.

"Now imagine back in 1955, here Dan and I are standing in front of the priest. I'm seventeen and I'm showing. The altar boys could barely keep their eyes off me and the Father was trying just as hard not to look at me. It was quite funny because we had Dave Krowell's sister, Adrianne, and her boyfriend stand up for us, and she was six months pregnant. Heads were turning everywhere. A week later we were all standing in front of the same priest and altar boys, only this time everything was reversed. Dan and I were standing up for Dave's sister as she married her boyfriend. We were all starting our new lives. Rock and Roll was just taking hold. I'm sure that the Father had a long talk with those young altar boys, railing on about the evils of the Devil's music.

"Those were the days of leather jackets, DA haircuts, cigarettes rolled up on your shirt sleeve and the bop. I felt very secure with Dan. He was big and strong and he and his group of friends were very protective of what was important to them. It's been that way our entire life together."

College

As with most local high school graduates, Dan enrolled at East Contra Costa Junior College, currently Diablo Valley College, in the fall of 1955 and played football under the coaching of Hal Buffa and Hugo Boschetti. That season he earned All-Conference honors.

"Loyalty was the key bond between all the Port Chicago boys. Ollie McClay, one of my good friends, had enlisted in the Army right after high school and when he returned home after his service was up, he attended ECC and became our halfback that season. We were playing Monterey and I got clipped pretty good and a fight started and the referee threw me out of the game for whatever reason. I became furious because I had to leave the field. At half time I snuck back onto the field just out of sight of the referee and watched as we were driving down the field to score. Ollie broke loose on one play and just before he was to cross the goal line, he side-stepped and ran right over the ref who had thrown me out of the game. He scored and as he was walking back to the sideline he looked over at me, smiled and gave me the thumbs up sign. Loyalty, that's what I'm talking about.

Nancy, Mindi and Me - Christmas 1957

"Nancy and I had our first child, Mindi, in December of that season. I did whatever I could to pay the bills and support my family. I cut lawns, worked in the canneries during the season and after classes most of the summer of 1956. I worked in the fertilizer plant in Nichols, a little town that's not here anymore. One of my good friends, Benny Venturino, came from Nichols. We were living in one of my aunt's homes in Port Chicago. It was a little hard but we were having fun. Mindi was the apple of my eye and Grandma Colchico's 'pet' for 21 years. We had some wonderful times; then Mindi left us for a long time."

Dan was voted into the East Contra Costa College, a/k/a Diablo Valley College, Sports Hall of Fame in 2008.

"I received a football scholarship to Southern Cal, but when I got down there to start the '56 season I saw all these kids driving around in new cars while I had two dollars in my pocket. I knew I would never fit in, so I left.

"I went up to the College of Pacific and they offered me a football scholarship. The week the season started I got a kidney infection and was gone for the season. I would have loved to play there and watch Dick Bass run.

"I thought my playing days were over so I returned to Port Chicago and took whatever job was available. I still had a growing family to take care of. It was then that a good friend of mine literally pulled me out of a bar. I thought a bunch of us guys were going to join the service. That friend of mine was former high school teammate Marv

McKean, who was the starting quarterback at San Jose State at that time. Marv stepped in and talked to San Jose's assistant football coach Gene Menges into taking a chance on me sight unseen. Coach Menges then talked to my JC Coach Boschetti.

When the time came for me to meet the coach, I took Clorets to hide my beer breath, put my cigarettes in my back pocket; I even tried to cover up all the fight scars with some makeup. I ended up getting a scholarship to play football at State. Everything changed right then. I thought about what my grandfather and Uncle Andy had said to me, 'You have to show people you deserve the opportunity they are offering you. Give everything you can. Never give up.' Like my father, it was time to pay back all those who had brought me to this point. That's why even when I was playing pro ball I hardly ever sat on the bench. You sit and you lose your job. I owe a lot to Marv and I thank him."

San Jose State 1957

Dan enrolled at San Jose State and started his three-year football playing career for The San Jose State Spartans under Head Coach Bob Titchenal. His number was 83. He won the starting job at both the offensive and defensive end positions.

The Spartans went 3 and 7 that first year, 1957, and Dan began to build his football legend right from the start. In the Denver University game, it was a victory for the Spartans, 27 to 20, on September 27th. Dan, along with quarterback Marv McKean, who also was a key player in the game, completed passes that set up two TD's and two extra points. Coach Bob Titchenal commented that Dan, "Repeatedly upset the Denver interference and forced the ball-carrier to stall on the run-pass option." This became Dan's trademark. No one wanted to run against Dan! He was very good at splitting a double team block.

"During this game, I didn't think about it at first because piling on after a tackle was common, and until the referee stopped it, it would continue throughout the game. My roommate was our guard, Herb 'Hubie' Boyer from Phoenix and as the game went on I started to notice that every time Hubie got knocked down or was involved in a tackle, more of the defensive players were piling on after the tackle. Well, one time I walked by and I heard Hubie yelling, 'Hey, guys, this is Denver, not Little Rock,' and it dawned on me what was happening. All I can say is, I started pulling people off him and I did it in such a way that it didn't happen again after that.

"It was also in this game that I saw, for the first time, racial animosity. I wasn't naive to what was happening around the country with the beginnings of the Civil Rights movement. But coming from a town like Port Chicago, which was a hodge-podge of just about all races, we really didn't think about it as a problem. Sure, we used certain words and names at times that may not have been appropriate but the bond between all of us made up for our lacking social graces. We believed in the old adage: sticks and stones may break my bones but names will never harm me. Sounds silly, but I believe too many people hide behind certain words to make up for their own shortcomings today."

In the San Diego State game on October 19th, Marv went down with the flu and did not play. Dan, with a knee injury, saw limited action. San Jose won this game 46 to 0 with backup quarterback Dick Vermeil completing a 67 yard TD pass. The next game against North Texas State would change the course of the season for both players and end the career for one of them.

At home on October 26th in a hard-fought but unremarkable game, North Texas State defeated San Jose State 12 to 6. The Spartan score came in the second quarter on a 52 yard pass from McKean to Ray Norton. While the game itself may have been less than spectacular, it was how the game ended after the final gun that made it memorable. Some observers called it, "the nastiest and lengthiest field fight" they had ever seen. Reported on Bruce Lee's sports page, "At mid-field, Colchico and three Texans suddenly began fighting. In eight seconds, both squads were in the melee. Ten policemen vaulted over the grandstand rail and waded in. Then a red-faced fan raced onto the field and hit Texas center Fred Way in the stomach. Way swung back, hit the fan in the face. Way swung on the cop. That did it - out came the billyclubs." Things quickly calmed down after that. What some had not noticed was that during the fight, a Texas player had snuck up beside McKean and punched him in the side of the face between the face guard and the rim of the helmet, knocking Marv to the ground. No one knew at that time what damage had been done to his face. The Texas players blamed San Jose center Ron Earl for starting the fight; somehow "Colchico evidently got in the way."

A few days later in practice Marv, his face swollen, spit out a piece of his cheek bone and that's when we all knew his face had been shattered. "Marv was never quite the same after that, and it ended his football days. He was as good as any of them and I feel he could have moved on. I know for a fact that the guy who sucker-punched him got paid back," states Dan, "and payback is a bitch!"

Passing duties after this incident fell into the hands of Mike Jones and future NFL Head Coach Dick Vermeil. Vermeil would coach the St. Louis Rams to a Super Bowl victory in 2000.

In Honolulu, November 30, San Jose State ended its season with a 12 to 0 victory over the University of Hawaii. In the Aloha Bowl game, Dan caught 6 passes for 86 yards. For his play this season, Dan was named All-American by the Williamson National Football Ratings System.

"Now I have a confession to make. I had a young wife and a small child to support. Back in those days there was very little financial support for college football players. The family always came first. I had to make some money.

"During the summer of '57, before starting the football season at State, I was asked by a long-time buddy of mine, Dennis Coffee, if I wanted to play a little ball for a semi-pro team he and some other local guys had started. The team was called the Alhambra Alumni Club Panthers, later to be changed to the CC Riders. I've known Dennis since we were 16 or 17 years old. We had played together on a number of different pickup teams for years. He was the quarterback and a darn good one my senior year at Mt. Diablo. Dennis was the Class of '56."

"The Riders had already played three or four games and they needed an end. As Dennis put it, 'Danny, I need an end with hands like yours who can catch the ball. The money's not that good but we make a buck or two.' So I said, 'Yes.' The problem was I couldn't use my real name. So while playing for the Riders, I was known as Leroy Vukad. What an adventure that summer turned out to be. We played on Saturdays or Sundays. We would play any team who would schedule us.

"So one day we are standing at the gate to San Quentin Prison, gear in hand looking up at the walls. The first thing that happened was the guards went through all our bags and took anything out made of metal, took our wallets, labeled them, put them in envelopes, stamped our hands just like they do when you went to a high school dance. Without that stamp you could not get out. Then they opened the gate and let us in and one of the scariest moments of my life happened. When they shut the gate and we all heard this loud clang, six inches of locked steel separated us from the outside. That's not a good feeling.

"We all dressed in the same room as the prisoners and that was a little frightening. Some of those guys were huge. We go out to the exercise yard to start the game and it was like a giant circus. The field was regulation size 100 yards by 40 yards and on the sidelines there were prisoners playing music, lifting weights and making bets, and at each end up on the wall were the guards with shotguns watching.

"We beat them, I think 21 to 6. We get on the bus to head home and Dennis says to me, 'I never want to go back there again.' Then he tells the whole team this story: He starts, 'Guys, I don't know if you noticed but I was talking to this prisoner in the dressing room and he tells me he's the quarterback for their team and he's betting on us to win. I look at him and say, okay, not certain how to respond to that. I continue talking, and ask him why he's here. He tells me he came home one day and found his wife and this guy together so he killed them both, and he said he was never going to get out of here. He also told me that most of these guys never played football before; they do it to have something to do.' We didn't make much money there and we never went back.

"In our last game in late August, we played the Oakland Athletic Club in the Pittsburg High Stadium and we beat them something like 35 to 14. I scored three touchdowns on passes from Coffee. Because I'm using an alias while playing for the Riders, the next day in Charlie Zeno's Post Dispatch column, the headline reads: Leroy Vukad Scored Three Times in Riders' Victory. Man, was he a hero. Leroy was our ticket sales guy; never played football in his life; had those big thick rimmed glasses. I'm glad we were paid in cash or I could never have cashed any of his checks. I made maybe 20 to 25 dollars a game, not much but it helped. Dennis, like any other quarterback, made the big money at about 50 bucks a game. Dennis can also play a mean piano, and back then he'd pick up a few bucks playing in some of the local honkytonks around Pittsburg.

"I played 14 football games in 1957; nine for State, five for the Riders (and family)."

The "C C Riders" at San Quentin

Coaches, Top Row Left: Leonard "Shams Pizza" Ciaramitaro, Anthony Pelligrini, Pete Lucido, 72- Joe Siino, 25 – Dan "Leroy Vukad" Colchico, 29 – Cliff Carpanello, 71 – Terry Taylor, 27 – Danny Gonzales, 17 – Chas Esposito, 41 – Martin DiMercurio, 71 – Bill Davis

Second Row: 66 – Jim Mulcay, 31 – Denny Coffee, 10 – Al "Coochy" Cassillas-- Blank Uniform- - 20 – George Moorhouse, 3 – Manuel Jiminez, 21 – Frank "Fongo" Aiello, 30 – Al Boot, 14 – No Name.

Front Row: Ed Miller, 12 – Chic Santoya, 11 – Frank "Pancake" Martinez, 61 – Pete Vienna, 16 – Mike Hurtado, 7 – Bob Ferraro, 22 –Bill Parnell no number.

"I was staying with friends that first season at State but when classes were over that spring of '58, I went back home during the summer. I took whatever jobs there were. I would sometimes work two jobs a day. I also worked out so I could put on a little more weight for the coming season.

"I first met Dick Boyd the summer before the '57 season. He was the Executive Secretary of the San Jose State Alumni Association, although he never attended State. We became fast friends. He arranged for housing for Nancy and me during the '58-'59 and '59-'60 seasons. Dick has played a very big part in my life. Stories will follow."

1958 - 1959 and a Touch from San Francisco

"Our first son Joseph was born in October of '58. Joseph grew into a big strapping boy, had some issues later on, but all turned out okay. We would go home to Port Chicago during the summers."

Nancy, Mindi, Joseph and Dan
Home – Port Chicago, 1959.

Just before the '58 season started for San Jose, a Sports Illustrated article in the September 22, 1958 issue stated that the Spartan offensive line will average 204 pounds this season with "Dan Colchico, a good receiver and blocker anchoring the right side." His coach, Bob Titchenal, tabbed the 6'4", 217-pounder as potentially the best all-around wingman on the Pacific Coast.

Some 45 candidates turned out for football in the fall. Dan, one of 12 returning lettermen immediately impressed the coaches. Titchenal stated that Dan, "Sure likes it when the going gets rough." Dan was named captain of the team.

The Spartans improved to a 4 win, 5 loss season in 1958, defeating Arizona State, Denver, Fresno State and Idaho.

In the Idaho game on November 1st Dan caught five third down passes and played a fine defensive game. For his performance, he was awarded the Wiley Smith Bag. Smith was an Examiner sports cartoonist who honored the area's outstanding college gridder each week with a traveling case.

When the season ended with a loss to Iowa State 9 to 6 on November 21st, Dan's season ending totals of 23 catches and 277 yards led the team in both categories. Then the honors started coming.

As predicted by Coach Titchenal, Dan was one of the best wingmen on the coast, being selected A.P. All-Coast Honorable Mention, A.P. Honorable Mention All-America, UPI Honorable Mention All-America, and was named the player who contributed most to the team. Not bad for a boy from the "wrong side of the tracks."

Then things got even better. Although Dan was a junior and still had one year of college eligibility left for the upcoming 1959 season, the San Francisco 49ers drafted him a "redshirt" as their seventh round pick in the 1959 draft.

Official Draft Program
San Francisco 49ers

NO.	PLAYER	POS.	HT.	WT.	SCHOOL
7B	Dan Colchico	E	6'4"	220	San Jose State

Future: Slot or closed end. Married. Good Size

Sports Illustrated reported in their September 21, 1959, issue that "despite strong support from sprinter halfback Ray Norton and end Dan Colchico, a good pro prospect, the San Jose Spartans face a dangerous schedule with a not-too-strong squad."

Things didn't go well at all for Dan in his 1959 senior year and last season with the Spartans. Although being named co-captain, Dan was injured for most of the year and the team finished with a 4 win, 6 loss record.

"I had a hip pointer most of the season. I got a combination shot of Novocain and Cortisone in my hip almost every day. The syringe looked like one of those football pumps and the needle a 10 penny nail.

"Now I'm going to call things the way I see them. The second smallest man I ever met in my life for lack of integrity and professional courage was our Assistant Coach Marty Feldman. I believe he had an ego beyond his abilities, and to prove his toughness he pushed players around as a coach. We had other injured players that year and his approach to practice and rehabilitation was one of, 'Do it my way. You will either play through it or we don't need you.' He broke some, and they were gone. I played during some practices and games not feeling my hips or legs, having no idea how much damage I was doing to my body. He would make comments, 'Look at Colchico, the pro; I don't know if he's going to make it.' He voted not to send me to the College All-Star Game. I think he, like a lot a former athletes who didn't make it to the pros or to whatever level he thought he should have, carried around that envy like an open book. And because of the position he had now would do anything to keep some players back. I think it gave him a feeling of superiority.

He went to the Oakland Raiders in 1961 and following the release of Eddie Erdelatz became head coach in September. Going 2 and 15 over the next two years he was dismissed and never coached again after that mess. I'll give him the credit he deserves for his service as a Marine in World War II, but football practice is not Boot Camp. I looked him right in the eye and I didn't bend.

"Then some good news came in November of that year. I was drafted fifth round by the Boston Patriots in the first draft by the new American Football League. I felt pretty good about that after having an off season, but I knew where my heart was I was going to stay home with San Francisco."

Dan was inducted into the San Jose State Football Hall of Fame in 1983. Dan was also named to the San Jose State All-Alumni Football Roster by the internet website Operation Sports Playmakers.

San Francisco – Kezar

The San Francisco 49ers, the first Major League Professional Sports Franchise in San Francisco, began to play professional football in the fall of 1946 as a charter member of the old All-American Football Conference which had been founded on June 4, 1944, by then Chicago Tribune's Sports Editor Arch Ward. Under founding co-owners Anthony "Tony" Morabito, his brother Victor, Allen E. Sorrell and E.J. Turre, the 49ers played their home games at Kezar Stadium and became one of the League's more successful teams.

In 1947 they obtained the rights to Army's two Heisman Trophy winners - Felix "Doc" Blanchard, "Mr. Inside 1945" and Glenn Davis, "Mr. Outside 1946." Blanchard did not play a professional game, but Davis went on to play for the Los Angeles Rams from 1950 to 1952. In 1948, 49er "Bootleg" quarterback Frankie Albert tied with the Browns' Otto Graham as League MVPs. In 1949, NFL Hall of Famer Joe Perry lead the League in rushing with 783 yards, and the 49er's Alyn Beals lead the league in scoring with 73 points. After placing second behind the Cleveland Browns in Division and Conference standings every year from 1946 to 1949 with a combined record of 38 wins, 15 losses and 2 ties, the 49ers, with Coach Lawrence T. "Buck" Shaw, and Assistant Al Ruffo, along with the Cleveland Browns and the first Baltimore Colts, were granted admission to the National Football League in 1950.

Shaw, born in Mitchellville, Iowa on March 28, 1899, was the assistant line coach and head coach at Santa Clara University from 1929 to 1942 where he compiled a 47 win, 10 losses and 4 tie record. Defeating Louisiana State in back to back Sugar Bowls in 1937 and 1938, Shaw was hired to coach the 49ers in 1944 for the sum of $25,000.

In that first NFL year, the 49ers went 3 and 9. Then over the next four years, from 1951 to 1954, the 49ers and Coach Shaw would win 30, lose 16 and tie 2. Shaw was fired in December 1954 and replaced by Norman "Red" Strader, a former 49er assistant coach and scout in 1952. In 1925, Strader became St. Mary's first football All-American. He would win 4 and lose 8 that 1955 season and was replaced by Frankie Albert in December of that year.

Albert was starting quarterback for the 49ers from 1946 to 1951. He led the AAFC in passing TDs in 1948 with 29 and also in 1949 with 27. Albert would lose his job to Y.A. Tittle in 1952. Albert was born on January 27, 1920 in Chicago, Illnois. He attended Stanford University, winning All-America honors in 1940 and 1941 and is enshrined in the College Football Hall of Fame. Some consider him the greatest left-handed quarterback of all time.

Albert's teams would win 19, lose 16 and tie 1 over the next three seasons. The 1957 season would be his best, going 8 and 4 and placing second in the conference. This season would be remembered for one major tragic event that occurred during their October 27th game with the Chicago Bears. The 49ers were trailing the Bears 17 to 7 when the team's beloved owner Tony Morabito collapsed in his 50 yard line seat and died of a massive heart attack. With tears running down his face, Coach Albert read the words to his team at half time telling them of their owner's death. "Tony's gone," he said. The 49ers scored 14 unanswered points in the second half and won the game 21 to 17.

The Detroit Lions defeated the 49ers 31 to 27 in the Western Conference playoff game to end San Francisco's historic year. Albert was released after going 6 and 6 in the 1958 season.

Red Hickey, Albert's assistant for the previous three years, became head coach for the 1959 season. The 49ers placed second in the Western Conference behind the Baltimore Colts. That year, with new players joining the team next season, Dan being among them, the 49ers looked forward to continued success.

John Gonzaga
49ers – 1955-1959

John was born in Martinez and grew up on the streets of Bella Vista, Bay Point. He was a local kid and the first Mt. Diablo High graduate to play professional football, Class of 1950. After high school he got a job at the local steel mill and began playing semi-pro sand lot football for the Martinez Alumni Panthers and other teams in the area. He was noticed by one of the scouts from the 49ers who offered him a tryout and, as they say, the rest is history. 1959 would be his last 49er season. He was moving on to the Dallas Cowboys then to the Detroit Lions from 1961 to 1965, and retired from the Denver Broncos in 1966. John played in over 130 professional games in his career. Dan and John became friends at an early age and remained so until John's passing in 2007. When Gonzaga was asked if he could give Danny any advice when he showed up at training camp, John stated, "Go to camp with intentions of making the club. Never give up. You can't afford to. That's how I got my job. Someone else let up and got the axe. I hung on." Dan's comment was, "John mentored me through my career."

During the off-season, before Dan reported to the 49er training camp, Ken McDonalds, Sports Editor for the Contra Costa Times, reported in his column "Time Out" on comments made by the publicity chief for San Jose State Spartans, Art Johnson. "Dan will make his mark among the pros as a defensive end or linebacker…He's 6'4" and should play at 245 pounds, and I may add, he's tough and nasty on the field. The tougher the going, the better he likes it…this Contra Costa native may just give the local fans something to shout about when the NFL season rolls around."

Rookie Dan Colchico 1960

"My first contract was for $7,500 of which $500 was a cash-signing bonus. It was handed to me by Lou Spadia. That averaged out to $625 per game. But that's not how we were paid. The team would divide the check by four, take the remaining 75 percent and divide that amount -- in my case $5,625 -- by twelve, the number of League games, and paid me $468.75 per game. After taxes, I took home $368, and I'm a professional football player! The remaining $1,875 was paid after the season, and that was paid without interest.

"Training camp opened for the rookies first and then seven days later the veterans reported. Training Camp lasted three weeks. Now, if you got cut before the first game you were usually billed for training camp expenses and sometimes they even billed the players who made the team! If you got injured and you did not make the team that was 'tuff luck.' You paid your own medical bills. Although the National Football League Players Association was started in 1956, they had very little power back then so there was very little recourse for any of our concerns. Most of us negotiated our own contracts.

"We played six exhibition games and were paid $50 per game for a total of $300 for ten weeks of training and exhibition games before the League season started. The federal minimum wage back then was $1.00 per hour for a 40 hour week, which adds up to $400 for ten weeks' work. So take $ 300 for ten weeks' work, or 400 hours, and that comes out to $.75 per hour. We were professional athletes but we sure weren't making a lot of money. Like my mother said, 'Be thankful you have a job,' and I was. For away games, our meal per diem was $9.00 per day or $3.00 per meal. If you worked at it, you could get a decent lunch or dinner for that amount because we were sure not staying at the Hilton. That was the life of most NFL players back then, or should I say the life of a 49er back then. I was lucky because my contact was larger than most as the minimum was $ 5,500. We all had jobs after the season to support our families."

The minimum wage today for a rookie who makes the team is approaching half a million dollars.

"It was late summer July 21st when I reported to training camp on the campus of St. Mary's in Moraga. It was hotter than hell and I knew what I had to do. I had to make the team or all the work that came before this moment would mean nothing. There were 27 rookies in camp and Coach Hickey was looking for linebackers. I, along with Rod Breedlove from Maryland, and others were being watched to see if we could fill the two open positions of middle and left side linebacker. The right side was filled by five-year veteran Matt Hazeltine, one of the best linebackers ever to play the game. I didn't care where they put me as long as I made the team. During that first week, I was moved over to the defensive end position and I fought it out with a kid from Utah State named Len Rohde. Rohde was a big, tough guy who would make a name for himself as an offensive tackle, making the Pro-Bowl in 1970 and playing for 15 years for the Niners, retiring in 1974. Some of those practices were an hour long with temperatures reaching over 100 degrees. We lost as much as tens pounds per session.

"Two days into practice, Coach Hickey stated, 'A lot of them (rookies) proved that they want to become 49ers,' and expressed particular satisfaction with the work of rookie Dan Colchico. We had two-a-day practices that included 30-minute scrimmages that seemed to go on forever, and back then I played both the right and left defensive end positions as well as special teams. I was dying out there. I finally asked one of our coaches, Mark Duncan, if I could take five. He said, 'Sure,' and I thought he meant five minutes. What he really meant was five breaths.

"During my rookie season at training camp we were told to write our name on a piece of tape and stick it on our helmet so he coaches would know who we were. The final cuts had not been made. I always gave 110 percent and the coaches and players knew it. A day or two after we had taped our name to the helmet, the offensive line coach, Bill 'Tiger' Johnson, stopped me and told me I could take off the tape. Both the offensive and defensive coaches knew who I was. I knew then that I had made the team."

Rookie Training Camp –
St. Mary's College, Moraga - 1960

Dan Colchico   Monte Clark   Leo "The Lion" Nomellini   Ed Henke
Matt Hazeltine   Bob "Hog" Harrison   Clancy Osborne

Hazeltine & Hickey   Defense: Harrison & Hazeltine

40-Woodson   55-Hazeltine
44-Dove   42-Ridion
80-Mertens   83-Kelley
70-Krueger   63-Clark
54-Harrison   73-Nomellini
86-Colchico

When Dan joined the 49ers in 1960, they still had three-quarters of the mid-1950's "million dollar backfield" - Hugh McElhenny, Y. A. Tittle and Joe Perry. The fourth quarter, John Henry Johnson had left for the Detroit Lions in 1957 and would be playing this year for the Pittsburg Steelers.

"I've known John Henry since I was a kid. He was from Pittsburg High right down the road from Port Chicago. In the late 40's he was the greatest athlete in the county; everybody went to see him play football, basketball and run track. He could do everything and do it well. To say he was fast is an understatement. He could jump, put the shot, even pole vault. He would win four or five events at all the track and field meets. I feel he could have been one of the greatest decathlon performers in any era. He would have given Bob Mathis a run for his money. He could even box. Y. A. Tittle commented, "I'm convinced if John Henry Johnson had been a prize fighter he would be heavyweight champion of the world because he did dish out punishment."

Tittle would leave for the New York Giants after this season, retiring in 1964. McElhenny moved on to the Minnesota Vikings in 1961 and retired with the Detroit Lions in 1964 after spending a year with his old teammate Y.A. in New York in 1963. Joe "The Jet" left for Baltimore in 1961 returning to retire with the 49ers in 1963. All four are in the NFL Hall of Fame.

"The first veteran I met that would become a good friend by season's end was Ed Henke. It was one thing to talk it up in the game and to kind of grab-ass a bit but I was still a rookie and I had not proven myself to all of them yet.

"After practice, many of us would go hunting for deer, quail and other game in the hills surrounding St. Mary's. There was a lot of open space and deer were all over the place. One evening after practice Ed Henke, St. Clair and I started cruising the dirt backroads behind the college in St. Clair's Cadillac convertible and we spotted some deer. We got out of the car and started walking but after awhile, having lost our opportunity, we started back. I had crossed the fence when I heard this unreal scream. I looked back and there was Ed, hung up -- no pun intended -- on the barbed wire fence. He had not only ripped a hole in his pants but had also ripped a gash in his scrotum. There was blood everywhere and the look on Ed's face - you thought he was going to die. We rushed back to camp and with Nomellini holding down one leg and Ted Connolly holding down the other leg, we stuck a towel in Henke's mouth. Then our two team doctors cleaned him up and sewed him up without Novocain. Ed then put a bag of ice in his pants and we left. He practiced the next day and played the following weekend. Like I said, you miss practice for some reason other than a game related injury and you lose your job. Ed got the handle 'one hung low.'"

Ed Henke came into Pro Ball out of USC in 1949, signing with the Los Angeles Dons of the old All-America Football Conference. After a short stay in the Canadian Football League in 1950 he signed with 49ers in 1951 and stayed until 1960, moving on the St Louis Cardinals and retired after the 1963 season.

"I remember well one other hunting excursion. It was a year or two later, after practice, when Bob St.Clair and I took this rookie from Kansas out behind St. Mary's and started driving through the hills. This rookie kept telling us he knew what a deer looked like. Now remember, this is private property with lots of ranchers raising cattle. We were in Bob's brand new 1962 Cadillac convertible when all of a sudden this rookie yells out, 'I see one; I see one.' I'm saying, 'Where?' The rookie keeps saying, 'Go back. I see one.' Well, he said he knew what he was doing so we back up and he says, 'I see one right there.' I say 'Okay,' and take him. Bang! From out of the dark we hear, Moo. The rest is history, as they say. There's more on this story in Bob's book, I'll Take It Raw!

"My first professional football game was somewhat of an historical event, not because I was playing my first game but because we were playing the new expansion team, the Dallas Cowboys, in that team's first-ever football game. It was the season's opening exhibition game in Seattle on August 6, 1960. In front of 22,000 fans we beat Tom Landry and Cowboy quarterback Eddie Lebaron 16 to 10. They played us tuff, but Dave Baker intercepted a pass with less than minute to play to end the game.

"It was also later in August that the line, 'wherever there is a brawl, you'll find Colchico' popped up. We were playing an exhibition game with the Philadelphia Eagles at Kezar and some time in the third quarter someone threw a punch and both benches cleared. The melee went on for over five minutes. Even our injured player, Max Fugler, who was standing on the sideline in civilian clothes, jumps in wielding a cane. The very next day in the Oakland Tribune's front page sports section, there's a picture of all this action and who's right in the middle? I can't hide anywhere.

"Our first league game of the season was against the New York Giants at Kezar on September 25th. Our starting middle linebacker, Bob 'Hog' Harrison, had injured himself in a boating accident before the season and couldn't play. Henke replaced him at the middle linebacker spot and they put Monte Clark at left defensive end. Monte was a better offensive tackle and that is where he made a name for himself later on. At the beginning of the second quarter they moved Clark to the right defensive tackle position, moved Charlie Krueger to right defensive end and put me at the left defensive end position right next to 'The Lion" Nomellini.

"Now that was something playing next to a legend. He called me 'kid' and I thought I was something special until I heard him call everyone kid. We called him 'Champ' because of his professional wrestling career."

Leo Nomellini, born in Lucca, Italy, started his wrestling career in the early 1950's in the San Francisco bay area during the off season from the 49ers. He wrestled for the NWA World Tag Team Championship. Leo won the Tag Team Championship, "The San Francisco Version," four times; the first one in March 1952 with partner Hombre Montana and again in May 1953 with teammate Rocky Brown. The third time was with Enrique Torres in May 1953 and finally again with Enrique Torres in May 1957. Then he traveled back to Minnesota where he had attended college and won "The Minneapolis Version" three times, with partner Verne Gagne in May 1958 and in July 1960. In between he won with team mate Butch Levy in July 1959. Leo won his last Championship in San Francisco in May of 1961 with partner Wilbur Snyder. When asked why he wrestled, he stated, "I make a lot more money doing that than I do playing football."

"We lost the game to the Giants 21 to 19. I would start every game the rest of the season, and I would start every game except for a few in my injury-plagued 1963 season, for the next four years.

"This was my rookie season and I wanted to prove to everyone on the team that I could do the job. We were playing a game at Kezar sometime in the middle of the year, and I got really pumped up. We were in our first or second defensive series when I jumped off-sides three times in a row. That gave them a first and ten then a first and five. We were back fifteen yards when Coach Hickey sends in Karl Rubke to take my place. I tell Rubke I'm not leaving. He just stands there and I tell him again, 'I'm not leaving.' He runs off the field. On the very next play I sack the quarterback for a 12-yard loss, and they punt. When the defense comes off the field, I walked by Hickey and said, 'I owe you three yards.' He doesn't look at me. On the very first play of our next defensive series I sack the quarterback for a four yard loss and they punt again. I walked past the coach again and told him, 'I was plus one in yardage.' This time he looked at me. I don't think he saw any humor in it.

"Monte Clark was my first roommate in the pros, a very big guy but he had these chicken legs. So on picture day he would take shin guards and put them in his socks so his calves would look bigger. He was very smart and worked hard to learn all about his position. We knew back then he could be a fine coach someday.

"Coach Hickey was a hard taskmaster with very strict rules. One rule was that you played with what you brought to the locker room on game day. If you forgot something that you needed to play with, well it could cost you your job. Krueger tells this story about a game in '59, Monte's rookie year.

"Krueger states, 'One Sunday, Monte looks inside his equipment bag and I hear this, Awe, shit! Clark had forgotten his shoes. I always carried two pair but mine were size 12 and he wore a 15. So he cuts off the front end of the shoes, sticks his feet in them, tapes over the entire shoe and uses shoe polish to make them look black. He played the whole game and Hickey was never the wiser.'

"The team's work week consisted of two-a-days, Tuesday through Friday and sometimes a practice on Saturday. Then if there was a home game, we would all check into the Burlingame Motel Saturday night. It didn't matter if you were married or not, everyone stayed there. We had Mondays off after a game.

"We were in Detroit to play the Lions on October 1st. Monty Stickles and I, both rookies this year, started to run around together almost from the first day of training camp. He and I were sitting in a little restaurant Saturday evening when Nick Pietrosante came in. Nick was the Lions' Pro-Bowl fullback. Sticks and Pietrosante knew each other from their playing days at Notre Dame, so Monty introduces me to Nick. He was a big kid, but what I remember to this day is that he gave me this limp two-fingered handshake. I don't know why but it just struck me as being a little different. I was all over Pietrosante that Sunday and we beat the Lions 14 to 10.

"In a memorable and historic game in Baltimore on November 27th the 49ers used Coach Hickey's new Shotgun Formation and defeated the Colts 30 to 22. John Brodie started the game but was removed after being injured by a ferocious hit by the Colts' defensive tackle, Big Daddy Lipscomb. Bob Waters took over from there and completed the victory.

"We were always looking for an advantage over the other team. We had not beaten the Colts since the last game of the '58 season so we wanted this one bad. St.Clair was banged up pretty good going into this game and we knew he would be in for one more of his legendary battles with the one and only Gino Marchetti. We had to devise a way to get Marchetti out of the game and do it legally. The coach sent in our center Frank Morze against Marchetti. Now Morze wasn't fast enough to catch my grandmother on the outside, but on the inside he was very good and strong. Marchetti did not like to be held so that's what we wanted Morze to do. Morze held Marchetti on three straight plays and Gino blew up and threw a punch at Frank. Both were kicked out of the game. St. Clair goes in and beats up on some rookie, and Waters remained safe for the rest of the game."

Gino Marchetti fought in the Battle of the Bulge in World War II. Afterwards, he went on to play semi-pro football for the Antioch Hornets in 1947, then to USF where he played with St. Clair on the "Undefeated, Untied and Uninvited" USF 1951 football team. Drafted 14th in the second round by the New York Yanks in 1952, and later that year coming to the Dallas Texans and becoming a Baltimore Colt in 1953. He remained with them until he retired in 1966. Eleven Pro Bowl selections, nine First Team All-Pro selections, two NFL Championships, and his number 89 was retired by the Colts. He was inducted into the NFL Hall of Fame in 1972, the Bay Area Sports Hall of Fame in 1985 and is a member of the National Italian American Sports Hall of Fame.

"Gino was a legend in Contra Costa County from his playing days at Antioch High from 1941-1943. I have known Gino most of my life, a great guy. After my rookie season some were comparing me to him as 'a young Marchetti, a new Marchetti on the block.' Well, let me state right here, Marchetti was one of a kind. Strong, fast, quick, both inside and outside, and big. We may have been in the same league together but he is in a class by himself.

"We went on to defeat Los Angeles 23 to 7 the following week and went into the December tenth game at home against Green Bay with a 6 and 4 record and a chance to take over the division lead. On a sloppy wet field we lost to the Packers 13 to 0. There was very little turf left on the field that Sunday as ours was the fifth game to be played there over that weekend. Called The Mud Bowl, I had my second encounter with Forrest Gregg and one more lesson of what it would be like to play in the NFL.

Dan mud wrestling with Jim Taylor on top of Nomellini – Dave Baker coming in for the kill with Krueger and Hazeltine looking on.

The "Mud-Head" centered behind is Forrest Gregg. Vince Lombardi stated "Forrest Gregg is the finest player I ever coached."

You can learn more about the great Forrest Gregg from his book titled "Winning in the Trenches – A Lifetime of Football"

"We beat Baltimore again in our last game at home on December 18th, 34 to 10, ending my first year in professional football. We finished 7 and 5 for second place behind leader Green Bay at 8 and 4. Our team defense rated number one in the League with the lowest total of points allowed, 205."

When asked why his team fared better this season than some had expected, Coach Hickey smiled and named off his six rookies: Mike Magac, Monty Stickles, Dee Mackey, Dan Colchico, Gordon Kelly, Bobby Waters and C.R. Roberts. "That's right, I include Roberts, too. He only played the last couple of games for us last year and he'd still be considered a rookie," stated the coach.

"Shortly after the season Pittsburg High held its annual Career Day Event. The great Jim Brown from the Cleveland Browns and I were guests of Joe Arenivar, Pittsburg's head football coach. Charlie Zeno was there conducting interviews for his daily column, when he asked Jim how he would rate the new kid on the block, Dan Colchico. 'One of the finest newcomers in the League and a leading contender for NFL Rookie of the Year Jim stated. 'Danny has one of the brightest futures of any rookie in the League. He plays the game all out, has the right attitude and stays in condition,' he continued. Wow, this from one of the greatest backs in history and throughout my career, one of the hardest backs to bring down.

"I received two votes and was runner-up for Rookie of the Year behind recipient Gail Cogdill of the Detroit Lions. Things were looking up, but I was still a rookie and I was not even invited to the end of the season team party. That would change though."

Some observations from on my first year in the League:
- The NFL is rugged; you face a tough, hungry player every game.
- You get hurt -- you play through it or go home.
- It's all about speed, how fast you can make a play happen.
- My teammate J.D. Smith, the hardest runner in pro ball but generally underrated.
He gained 780 yards this year after coming off his all-pro year of '59 with 1036 yards.
- Nomellini was the greatest lineman ever.
- Tittle is still a great quarterback.
- Brodie needs to play more to reach the top.
- McElhenny, The King, don't understand why "Mac" was waived to Minneapolis.
- Hornung could do it all.
- Taylor very good.
- Lipscomb good -- but not in the same class as Nomellini.
- John Brodie never liked the Shot Gun formation. John said after the season, "I hate to run, I run like fourth class mail. Pro teams with good running quarterbacks never win." St. Clair called John a "pure drop back pocket passer, who could have been in the Hall of Fame if we, the 49ers, had won a few playoffs or championships. Back then all the media was back east and nobody knew who Brodie was.

"The year had gone along well, I thought but not completely without some team discontent. McElhenny, who had problems with the coaching staff the last two years, was sold to Minnesota. Henke, my good friend, wanted out, so he was traded to St. Louis. They traded Tittle to New York for Lou Cordileone. This made room for Brodie, which worked out very well for both of them. They let 'The Jet' Joe Perry go to Baltimore after 12 years of service."

FIRST ROW, left to right: Henry Schmidt (trainer), Dave Baker, Abe Woodson, Jerry Mertens, Bob Harrison, Matt Hazeltine, John Brodie, R. C. Owens, Tommy Davis, Jim Ridlon, Billy Wilson, Chico Norton (equipment manager). SECOND ROW: Joe Perry, Bob Waters, Eddie Dove, Clyde Conner, Y. A. Tittle, J. D. Smith, Hugh McElhenny, Leonard Lyles, C. R. Roberts. THIRD ROW: Jack Christiansen (assistant coach), Karl Rubke, Charlie Krueger, Len Rohde, Ted Connolly, Bruce Bosley, John Wittenborn, Mike Magac, Ray Norton, Clancy Osborne, Monty Stickles, Mark Duncan (assistant coach), Howard Hickey (head coach). FOURTH ROW: Henry (Hawk) Schmidt, Ed Henke, Gordon Kelley, Monte Clark, Captain Bob St. Clair, Dee Mackey, John Thomas, Frank Morze, Leo Nomellini, Dan Colchico.

1960 was also the first year for the new American Football League franchise team from across the bay, the Oakland Raiders. Oakland would upstage the 49ers in the late 60's by going to Super Bowl II in January 1968, and losing to the Green Bay packers 33 to 14. That team was coached by John Rauch and quarterbacked by the legendary "Mad Bomber" Daryle Lamonica. "I would play in a lot of Lamonica's golf tournaments over the coming years, starting in 1968 in the first Lamonica invitational tournament at Round Hill Country Club, Alamo, California."

Now with the season over, what to do and where to find a job? "I knew I couldn't just lay around and wait for next season to start. Nancy looked at me one evening at home and commented, 'Dan, now that you're a big-time professional football player, don't you think we could get a little better place to live?' Hell, I was perfectly happy with our cozy little three-room house. 'Of course, dear,' I said, and we bought a three-bedroom house down the street; a bedroom for us and two extra for our growing family.

"It was very nice to be home and make the rounds again, stopping at the local joints and getting caught up on the town's gossip: Tony Madrazo's "Bank Club", Walt and Ruth Hegarty's "Walt's Inn" and one of my favorites, George Sarris's the "Sarris Saloon." George never carded anybody. Then over to Martinez and drinks at George Grilli's place and a final at Leo Pecciante's Angelos.

"I took a job selling cars for Jorgensen Ford in Pittsburg that summer. I had house payments now and I did pretty well, selling 36 new Fords and 47 used cars that first year. And not bad money. My slogan, 'I'll work just as hard to get you the best deal as I do on the football field.'

"In between jobs and family, I was invited to numerous banquets, honorary dinners, testimonials and awards ceremonies. The Concord Elks Lodge started a yearly 49er Honorary dinner. The Port Chicago Lions Club started an annual Sports Night; the Concord Quarterback Club began to invite 49er players over to give talks at dinners and roundtable discussions. This was what I always wanted. Now, my hometown friends and I could share some of the success we all achieved and I believed that, without the support of all my 'gang,' it wouldn't have been as much fun. "My hometown of Port Chicago gave me two such dinners. The first on January 18, 1961, sponsored by the Port Chicago Lions and the HenryMorken Post of the American Legion. They honored me and San Francisco Giant catcher Hobie Landrift. Long-time friends Elsio DeMarco, Jim Eliason, Walter Gandera, Earl Caudill and Manuel Nunes were the working committee.

"The second Colchico Appreciation Night, chaired by my old high school teammate, Larry Reece, was held February 4th at the Town House in Port Chicago. Master of Ceremonies was Charlie Zeno, a great friend of mine and sports editor for the Pittsburg Post. One of the speakers was Rod Franz, my former high school coach, who made the comment during his talk, 'When Dan came out for football, I gave him a week to ten days I thought he could make last string on the JV team. Then one day I held a blocking bag for him and from the way he jarred my molars I knew he was going to be a Pro player.'

"The guests included 49ers Eddie Dove and Monte Clark former 49er and now Dallas Cowboy, local boy John Gonzaga and Jack Larscheid of the Oakland Raiders. I met Jack when I went to UOP.

Jack related this story to the audience: I was working out one day at Pacific when Danny came over and said he had just come back from USC where they had 11 strings on their football team and he had made it up to third string before he left. He figured he could do better at Pacific and asked if I could put in a good word for him with Coach Jack 'Moose' Myers. Well, Dan joined the team but soon thereafter he's in the hospital getting an appendectomy. The following season in '57 we played San Jose State. There is Dan on the sideline and on the first team. At the pre-game pep talk Coach Moose said, 'We've got his appendix; now I want you guys to get his legs.'

"All I can say is that they did a pretty good job on me because Jack and the rest of the Tigers beat us 21 to 6. Bert Ravizza, Elsio and Leo DeMarco, Frank Delaganese. Paul Lange and Gordy Powell, all hometown buddies were the working committee for this event. We had a ball.

"It was also at the end my first season, starting in the spring of 1961, that I began my own speaking engagements and Master of Ceremonies duties. I spoke at the Holy Name Society dinner at Queen of All Saints School in Concord and at the Concord Quarterback Club, to name a few."

The City

(*Dan's story, in his own words*)

I had been introduced to the San Francisco North Beach nightlife in 1957 when my friend, Dick Boyd, who had helped Nancy and me get housing when I was at State, started taking me to some of the better known joints in "Little Italy." Places like the North Beach Café owned by Ernie and Walt Lagomarsino, which was across the street from boxing promoter Joe Caparole's Capp's Corner. The "Beatniks," a term coined by Herb Caen in 1958, were still in fashion; the hippies and topless bars were a few years away. In 1960 and being a 49er, a lot of doors were beginning to open. Things really took off in 1961 when Dick opened Pierre's with his partner Maurice Bessiere, at the corner of Broadway and Romolo in 1961.

Our routine after home games was clean up and head to the local watering holes. Our first stop was the Shadow Box on California for a few cold ones to get the hurt out. Then down to Brodie's and St. Clair's favorite spot, the 622 Club on Green Street, for dinner. After a few more, it was off to Pierre's.

Once in awhile during the week Len Rohde and I would go down to this little place in North Beach called the Red Garter. A couple of times we stayed a little longer than was practical and the practice next day hurt a little more than usual. In '64 when the Condor Club opened, we would stop by and, more often than not, find St. Clair ready and willing to buy a round. Of course, after 1961 Billy Kilmer was always around, too.

We had this kid named Mike Lind, drafted out of Notre Dame, come to the 49ers as a fullback in '63. Mike was big and strong and, like most fullbacks, full of fun. During a special promotion, The Condor Club had a young 3'11" doorman named Herve Villechaize -- yes, that guy "Tatto" from Fantasy Island fame in the '80's. One Sunday after a home game in '64, Mike and I and others started our usual swing though town ending up at the Condor. I don't remember how it started, but for some reason Lind and Villechaize got into an argument. The conclusion was that Mike stuffed Herve into a garbage can. Great fun. No one hurt, right? Well, I guess Villechaize didn't take it that way.

We were back home two weeks later after another home game and we started our routine, and late in the evening we're back at the Condor Club. Here is 3'11" Villechaize, staring up at 6'2" Lind. We all figure this will end up just like the first time. Then Villechaize pulls out a short barrel revolver, sticks it under Mike's chin, and says, "If you ever try to do what you did before, I'll blow your head off," and he was not kidding.

Years later you can laugh about what happened but it sure cooled that night. Villechaize would kill himself with a revolver in 1993.

Pierre's became one of the team's more popular night spots over the next few years, for after-practice relaxation and post-home game celebrations or for easing the pain after a loss. You never get over a loss but a few cold ones help relieve the soreness of strained muscles and a broken finger or two. Dick had a 49er special. The general public paid one dollar for draft beer; we got the same 12 ounces for fifty cents.

Dick wanted to turn his place into a sports bar to attract local professional athletes and the fans who wanted to rub elbows with the star of the day. He had Ladies Night almost every night and wasn't against keeping a few of the, let's say, friendlier ones around at the bar as in house attractions. Charlie Krueger, Matt Hazeltine, St.Clair, Monty Stickles and Billy Kilmer and I were regulars. Brodie, Nomellini, and others would show up from time to time; it was pretty much a 49er hangout. We had this rookie, Dave Kopay, a running back out of Washington in 1964. He would come in, sit at the bar with us and if there was a new bartender on duty he would never get served because he looked 16, not 22. He would just sit there, and then finally ask, "What about me?" He would have to show his ID and the rest of us would have to vouch for the fact that he really was a 49er so he could get his fifty cent beer. We nicknamed him "Psycho." He weighed about 195, maybe 200, and in practice he came at you with this fierce abandon. Three or four of us would knock the crap out of him. He'd lay there a second or two, get up walk back to the huddle and do it all over again. He never quit. Then one day at the start of one of our games we were passing and he came up to me and asked, "Dan, please don't call me Psycho anymore, I never really liked it." Dave retired from football with the Green Bay Packers in 1972. In 1975 Dave came out as being gay. Some years later at a banquet held for some of us old 49ers, Dave and I were having a conversation. I shook his hand and told him, "You have no problem with me." Pro ball being what it was back then, it took a lot of personal guts to stand up for who he was.

Members from other teams who came to town to play us would show up at Pierre's every now and then, especially some of the Packers. Boyd Dowler and Max McGee came in from time to time. I had few drinks with Paul Hornung.

Max was quite a guy and one hell of a receiver. He was also known for breaking team curfew rules from time to time. He had spent two years in the Air Force so he knew how to get around. Max had a rather poor 1966 season due to injuries and creeping age, catching only four passes all year. The Packers won the NFC Championship that year with a 12 and 2 record and would be playing the Kansas City Chiefs in Super Bowl 1 in January 1967. McGee, thinking he wouldn't be playing in much of the game, stepped out on the town the night before the game.

In the locker room, before the start, Max tells starting end Boyd Dowler, "I'm not in real good shape, don't get hurt." Well, Dowler goes down on the second drive of the game and Lombardi sends in McGee. Max had to borrow a helmet from a teammate before he could go on the field that's how certain he was he would not be playing. A couple of plays later McGee becomes a Super Bowl legend, making a one-handed catch of a Bart Starr pass and running 37 yards to score the first TD in Super Bowl history. By the end of the game, Max had caught 7 passes for 138 yards and two touchdowns. He would become the Packers color commentator for their football games from 1979 to 1998, retiring in '99 to found the Max McGee National Research Center for Juvenile Diabetes. Max died of an unfortunate accidental fall in October 2007. He was one of Lombardi's favorite players.

I don't know why but very few SF Giants came in. Wilt Chamberlain from the Warriors showed up often. He was a hell of a guy and, as he has stated himself, quite the ladies' man.

Stickles worked as the doorman and bouncer off and on over the years. When it turned 2:00 a.m., Dick would lock the door and Nancy and I, with other couples, would hang around sometimes until eight or nine o'clock, have breakfast, then go home. Remember, we had Mondays off. On one particular night some of the local, let's say, keepers of the peace came in about 3:00 a.m. John Mellekas and I, and a couple of the lawmen, had a little target practice on some of the bottles on the back wall. We got away with it. We had a little cover that night.

Dick closed his place down sometime in 1965 after the topless and strip joints started opening up. It's not that Dick didn't appreciate adult entertainment; hell, his first waitress was Margo St. James and we all know what she started! He just didn't like what the area was turning into. There is a difference between a "doorman" and a "barker" and Dick had a doorman. To him there were too many barkers, street hustlers, and otherwise seedy individuals coming into his beloved North Beach, changing the flavor of this once tight-knit community. Forty years later Dick published the book "Broadway, North Beach. The Golden Years, A Saloon Keeper's Tales." If you want to know what North Beach was all about in the 50's and 60's this is the book for you.

By the way, Margo, whatever people might say about her, was a really fine person. She opened a lot of doors so that others could reach their potential. She will forever be an icon of that '60's San Francisco mystique.

Season 1961 – The League Season Expanded to 14 Games

Six pre-season games at $50 per game, $300 total pay. Tittle was coming back to San Francisco as the quarterback for the New York Giants in a pre-season game at Kezar. Well, I missed the team lunch before the game and was fined $50. The thought of playing the game for nothing enraged me. I played like a madman and we won the game 42 to 10. I received the game ball and my money back. I was a professional. That $50 belonged to me. We made money the old-fashioned way. We earned it! The game was rougher, more dangerous than it is today. A player could crack back block, spear with his helmet; the quarterback could be hit at any time or any place on the field. You didn't sit out because you were tired or hurt.

We started off the regular season with a fine 4 win, 1 loss record defeating the Washington Redskins in the opening game on September 17th at home. We lost to Green Bay away, then won three in a row over Detroit, the Rams and Minnesota. With nothing left in the tank, we got clobbered by the Chicago Bears 31 to 0 on October 22nd in Chicago. After this loss, Coach Hickey lost confidence in the Shot Gun offense and basically shelved it. We used it very little after that. We lost two out of the next three games with 1 tie.

We all know that football is a violent bruising sport, but did you ever stop to think about how dirty the players get when playing the game? I'm talking about the physical dirt and grime a player gets on his body by sweating though a three and a half hour game. Until Astro Turf came along, we played on a grass-covered dirt field, sometimes dust dry, other times in three inches of mud, or six inches of snow with the wind blowing in all directions. You are standing there on the scrimmage line, guys are dripping sweat, blowing their nose, bleeding, spitting on the ground. Hell, some players have even been known to relieve themselves standing in the huddle. But you never think about this stuff when in the heat of battle. You get knocked down, stomped on, run over. When four or five guys are on top of you, you really don't think about what you're laying in, but sometimes when it gets quiet, well, the "Ick factor" comes into play.

In one of the games we were playing early in the season, I don't recall which one, I was standing on the sideline watching the offense and this passing play goes all wrong. Clyde Conner, our split-end, runs off the field and I ask him what happened. Clyde tells me, "You know how Brodie is always picking his nose, we're in the huddle and there's John, with his finger up his nose and he's calling a passing play. Just as we are about to break, I tell John, don't throw the ball to me! Everybody started to laugh and the play never did come off right. That was Conner's "*ick* factor."

On Sunday October 29th I was the cover story for the San Jose Mercury News Sports Page, titled "Ready for Work" by Dan Hruby; it was the local boy makes good story. He reported on our second victory of the season on October 1st over the Detroit Lions in Detroit. We defeated them 49 to 0. In that game I tackled Earl Morrall for a 12 yard loss right at the end of the first half and we were leading 21 to 0 at the time. They never recovered. I got a "nice play, Colchico" from Hickey the following Tuesday at the film review meeting. I went off to the whirlpool and fell asleep; had to get ready for the two-a-days tomorrow. I wouldn't have it any other way.

Billy Kilmer was in his rookie year, just out of UCLA. He and I became fast friends. On our days off I pulled him along on some of my local charity events. We attended the championship awards ceremony on Monday, November 13th for the Pittsburg Mallards of the Eastbay Pop Warner Football League, just after our loss to the LA Rams. Billy and I had a great time and the kids were awe-struck. Over the next few years we would do a lot more of these events.

Billy was drafted for his running ability from the quarterback position. It was rumored that he was the shot-gun quarterback and that Brodie was going to be traded. He had a good rookie season rushing for over 500 yards with a 5.3 yard average and passed for 280-plus yards. In '62 he was used mostly at left-halfback gaining close to 500 yards with a good 5.1 yard average. But '62 would end very badly for Bill.

After our mid-season four game run of 3 losses and 1 tie we beat Chicago on November 19th at home and came back the next week to defeat the Vikings again at home on November 26th.

We were coming off a loss to Baltimore on December 3rd, when we played Green Bay the next Sunday, the 10th, at home. Green Bay was the first team to beat us this season. They had beaten us five times in a row going back to 1959. Late in the game, I crushed Bart Starr, just as he was releasing the ball and it floated into the hands of our defense back, Jimmy Johnson, who returned it some 60 yards to the Green Bay 12 yard line. We won the game 22 to 21.

After the game, Coach Hickey commented, "Danny is a 120 percent guy, a player who still gives a little bit more after he's given an all-out effort. A great second-effort guy who never quits trying. He has not played a bad game all year." Wait until contract time, I'm thinking.

Baltimore beat us 27 to 24 at home on December 16th, ending our season at 7 wins, 6 losses and 1 tie for fifth place in the League.

Comments on my second season in the NFL:

Green Bay's Jim Taylor, Cleveland Browns' Jimmy Brown, Baltimore Colts' Lenny Moore, and LA Rams' Jon Arnett were the hardest backs to bring down in the League. I still rate our own J.D. Smith with the best, and that goes for Paul Horning with Green Bay. John Brodie was the most underrated quarterback in the NFL. In fact, I think he's the best right now in the League. I don't remember Billy Wilson ever dropping a ball.

Our second son, and third child, Dominic was born in February of 1962. Dominic was always a good student. He received his BA degree in Criminal Law from the University of Nevada. He later went on to work for our third son, Matthew, in the janitorial business for approximately 7 years.

"Colchico Den"
1962

Nancy holding newest son Dominic, with Dad and Joey showing off the football to Mindi.

Back home after the season, I'm still selling cars and attending all those sports dinners.

The Concord Elks Lodge #1994 held its first annual Sports Appreciation Night on May 17, 1962. I brought a number of 49ers over to talk about the previous season and football in general. Co-chairs Gene Keefe and Don DeRosa sold 470 tickets at $2.00 apiece. Fatts DeMartini and Eddie Gomes were the evening chefs. Gordy Soltau, former 49er, was Master of Ceremonies. Teammates attending were Billy Wilson, John Brodie, Ted Connolly, Jerry Mertens, Frank Morze, C. R. Roberts, Monte Clarke, Ed Henke, Don Burke, Alyn Beals, Eddie Forrest, Bob St. Clair and team trainer Henry Schmidt. Some of the evening's comments:

Bruce Bosley said, "As far as I'm concerned, one player didn't go to the Pro-Bowl who was deserving, and that's Dan."

Monte Clark, "I heard he was a rough and tough football player and his play has proved it."

Bob St. Clair, "I had to contend with 'Mad Dog Henke' for years in practice and when Danny came up as a rookie I thought I'd get a rest. But Danny belted me in the mouth in the first scrimmage and right then I knew we had a football player with the same attitude as Henke."

But what touched me the most was what my State Coach, Bob Titchenal had to say… "Dan is one of the finest athletes San Jose State ever had. He worked hard in college with a wife and his two children, Mindi and Joe, to support. He developed from an ordinary guy into a fine gentleman, but he's still a tough kid who can play football in any league."

The evening was such a success that the Lodge continued to honor 49er players for a number of years.

Gordie Soltau played for the 49ers from 1950 retiring after the 1958 season. In the nine seasons with the team he led them in scoring with 644 points, made All-Pro three times, three Pro-Bowls appearances and led the NFL in scoring in 1952 and '53. In 1954 he became the 49ers first Players Representative in the New Players Association earning the nickname "The Senator."

After retiring, Gordie went on to broadcasting for CBS Television for the next ten years, and then joined Lon Simmons at KSFO radio for five years. Gordie is an inductee in the Minnesota Hall of Fame and was inducted into the "Bay Area Sports Hall of Fame" in 1999.

1962 Winning On The Road – Losing At Home

We would do anything within the rules to win a game. Pre-season games back then were taken a little more seriously than they are today. We played to win - always. I had dislocated my knee in practice on Thursday, but I wanted to start. The team trainer had this liniment - everyone called it snake oil. It was actually Menthol Sulfide. I rubbed it all over my leg and knee. It had a tingling and cooling effect but for some reason it also made my breath smell like a garlic and sulphur mix.

I lined up on defense and all I heard was, "G—D---, Dan, what in the hell did you eat?" We won the game and afterward in the clubhouse, Hazeltine says, "Colchico asphyxiated the entire offense line." Sometimes we would put it on even if we weren't hurt.

With our backfield of Brodie, J. D Smith and Kilmer intact and the defensive line still together, it was looking good going into '62, but we couldn't win at home.

We dropped the first two games of the season, first at Kezar to Chicago, 30 to 14, then in Detroit to the Lions 45 to 24. In the Detroit game with the Lions leading 31 to 24 in the fourth quarter, Kilmer took a pass from Brodie and carried it 60 yards to the ten yard line, then promptly fumbled it only to have a Lion recover it. Billy went from hero to goat in one play according to the papers the next day.

In what turned out to be the best game of the season for the hometown fans at Kezar on September 30th, we beat Minnesota 21 to 7. At the time we didn't know it would turn out to be our only hometown victory.

It's during this time that my crazy cousin Donnie was attending a home game at Kezar Stadium. He had just returned from a tour of duty with the Army and was eager to see me play. I looked up from the field and saw a large commotion, when suddenly a huge cloud of red smoke began billowing up from the grandstand. Someone had apparently set off a smoke bomb. After the game I met Donnie and Nancy in the parking lot and before I could say a word, he stated, "Yeah, it was me. I wanted to clear the stands so I could see the game!" Well, he got what he wanted as people with red clothes, hair and hats had quickly cleared the area. Luckily, Nancy was seated with the other wives on the opposite side of the stadium.

On the road October 7th we beat Baltimore 21 to 13. He went to Chicago the next week and defeated Mike Ditka and the Bears 34 to 27. On October 21st, at Lambeau field, we lost to the Packers 31 to 13. This game was the first of a four game losing streak. The next three at home: LA Rams, 28, 49ers 14, Colts, 22, 49ers, 3, Detroit, 38, 49ers, 24.

At the LA Coliseum November 18th I had one of my better games chasing Jon Arnett around the field and we beat the Rams 24 to 17 to start a three game winning streak.

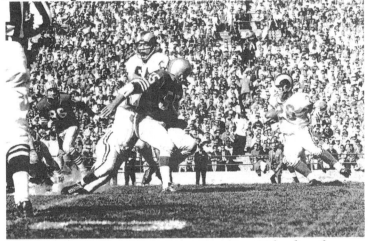

I've got Arnett in my sights... Hazeltine 55 leading the way...

We defeated the St. Louis Cardinals and the Vikings on the next two Sundays on their own fields. We stand 6 and 6 and go back home for our last two games.

Then Hornung, Taylor and the rest of the Packers come to town and beat us 31 to 21. Jim Brown picks up the ball the next week with the

Cleveland Browns and ends our season on a losing note, 13 to 10. Six losses, one win at home; five wins, two losses on the road; fifth place in the League.

I had faced some very tough and hard running backs those last three years. Jim Taylor of the Packers and Jim Brown of the Browns led the pack. But after the Cardinals' game, I put John David Crow right up there with those two. I ached the entire week after that game. I was sure glad he came to us a couple of years later.

"It was after the last game of the season with Cleveland that the team notified me that I had been awarded the Len Eshmont award as the team's "Most Inspirational Player" for that season. It's the greatest thing that had ever happened to me as a football player. I was also given a $1,000 watch which I gave to my mother. She was so proud of that watch. When she would meet new people she'd say, "This is a $1,000 watch my son gave it to me. See this dress I'm wearing. I paid $3.95 for it." Typical for immigrant-raised mothers back then, proud of their family's accomplishments, yet humble at the same time.

Leonard "Len" Eshmont played professional football, first for the New York Giants in the NFL, right out of Fordham University in 1941. After World War II he joined the 49ers of the old All-American Football Conference in 1946 and retired after the 1949 season. Len died of infectious hepatitis in 1957.

The award given in his name each year is to the player who best exemplifies "inspirational and courageous play throughout the year." It is voted on by the player's teammates and is considered one of the highest honors a player can receive.

At the Seventh Annual 49er Luncheon hosted by the Gent Chefs and held at the Claremont Hotel in March of '63, I was presented a watch by the Gent Chefs as the most valuable player for the season. The Gent Chefs were a group of local businessmen who got together and hosted lunches and dinners honoring the areas pro teams. The food was okay, but the water highballs were damn good.

Mindi, Joseph, Matthew and Dominic – Back yard, 1966

Nancy and I had our fourth child in April of '63, son Mathew. Matt was the typical teenager. He'd ask his mom, "Where's my clean underwear?" Nancy would respond, "I don't know. I see some dirty ones on the floor at the end of your bed. I don't have any to clean in the hamper." It took a while but he caught on. He graduated from Cal Poly and he runs his own janitorial service. Cleanliness is next to Godliness and can make you money, too.

1963 Injuries
Nomellini and St. Clair Retire

At the beginning of the season we were looking for a better year than our 6 and 8 record in '62, but we never got our offense working. Billy Kilmer, a starter, backup quarterback and halfback who had played a good deal of football in '61 and '62, rushing for over 1000 yards, had nearly killed himself in a car crash in December of '62. He pushed two bones through his lower leg and missed the entire '63 season. The quarterback position was split between John Brodie and Lamar McHan. We lost our first three games to the Vikings, Colts then the Vikings again. To make things worse, John went down with a season-ending injury. That turned the offense over to Lamar McHan, our third team quarterback, who had come over from the Colts in the off season. After we lost our first two games of the season, it was reported in the Contra Costa Times on September 27th that I might be traded to the Los Angeles Rams for Zeke Bratkowski. We needed a quarterback. Brodie was gone so it made sense, but I'm glad it didn't happen. The offense was so bad that the joke among the defensive players was that our offensive series consisted of, 1 fumble, 1-2 interception, 1-2-3 punt, and Brodie would line up over the center to then signal for a "fair catch."

For some reason, when Billy was placed in the hospital, the team placed him off limits which meant only his family could visit him. I think management thought we might hinder his recovery. So one evening Matt Hazeltine, Bruce Bosley and I found our way into the hospital, found an employees' lounge, found some long white hospital coats and a couple of clipboards. We started to inspect some of the patients' rooms. No one stopped us or even asked what we were doing. Of course, we found Kilmer and he looked like hell. An hour or so later he looked a lot better and I can tell you, he sure felt a lot better.

Bill thought his career was over because of this injury, so when he got out of the hospital he went home in Southern California and started working in his dad's dry cleaning business. One day a bunch of us guys walked into his dad's shop and there Billy was pressing a pair of pants. He looks up at us and says, "This isn't for me." He takes off his apron and tells his dad, "I'm done," and walks out.

Bill started to work out again and he was back in camp for the '64 season. But he saw very little playing time in '65 and after a contract dispute in '66 the team put him in the '67 NFL Expansion Draft. He was picked up by the New Orleans Saints and played there from 1967 to 1970. I would join him there in my last two seasons of 1968 and 1969."

Kilmer would move over to the Washington Redskins and play from 1971 until he retired after the 1978 season. He led the Skins to an 11 win, 3 loss seasons in 1972 and then lost to the undefeated Dolphins 14 to 7 in Super Bowl VII in January 1973. Billy had a great career and we have remained friends to this day.

I had just come off a good year, winning the Eshmont Award and was looking for another good season. Statistically '63 was one of my better years. Because the defense was on the field so much of the game I tied with Abe Woodson for most fumbles, recovered with four and raised my tackle totals.

My first football trading card came out this year - Topps # 144. I thought that was pretty neat. We didn't make any money from this. We just signed the paper so they could use our picture. I heard later on that the baseball guys where getting the unheard of amount of $5.00 to sign the contract to use their names. They called this "steak money" because you could buy a steak dinner for that amount. Well, I sure didn't get any this year or in '64 either. I've been told that my cards are being offered on E-Bay for a buck and a half apiece and one guy is asking $300 for one in mint condition. If I had thought ahead, I could have saved some. Well, someone's making money!

We started the season at home losing to the Minnesota Vikings 24 to 20. So back in camp the following week, in one of our X and O meetings, Coach Hickey was showing us his diagrams on the chalkboard about how we were out of place and didn't make the tackles quick enough. Well, he wrote this big X over the defensive tackle position and he became so intense that he broke his piece of chalk. Continuing to face the board, he picked up another piece and he began to draw a circle around the X and he kept saying, "And our defensive tackle never got out of the circle; our All-Pro defensive tackle never got out of the circle." He broke another piece of chalk and still facing the board he picked up one more piece of chalk and now he's pounding the board with the chalk and he kept saying, "Our G__ D__ All-Pro defensive tackle never got out of the circle all game." The chalk shatters. We are all sitting there saying nothing. We all know who he is talking about, the Champ, Nomellini. Nomellini never blinked and never said one word.

Four weeks later we are playing the Baltimore Colts in Baltimore and they have this offensive player, whom you probably have heard of, named Lenny Moore. He could come at you from the backfield or the wide receiver position, and there weren't many players in the League faster than him. The one thing that most didn't understand about Nomellini was that he was a lot faster than he appeared. He could never catch Moore from behind but if he got the right angle he could get you. So on one play I called a cross play where I went inside and Leo went to the outside. Moore was running down the sideline and Nomellini had the angle and about 30 yards down field, Moore cut to the inside. That's when Leo got him and got him good and I, trailing behind, piled on. We got up and I heard the PA announcer, "Tackle made by Nomellini, assisted by Colchico." Man, I loved that! As we are walking back to the line, Leo pulls on my jersey and says, "Hey, kid, I guess I got out of the F-----g circle that time." I loved piling on. I loved hearing, "tackle by Colchico." We lost this game 20 to 3. This was our fifth loss in a row, as we had lost the previous week in Detroit to the Lions 26 to 3.

Nomellini was one of the great guys on the team and just like John Gonzaga he had this natural strength. He was the strongest man I ever met and he never lifted weights.

At half time at home we were losing to Baltimore in the second game of the season. The team was already on the field to start the second half but Monte Stickles had left his helmet inside and went back to get it. Just as Coach Hickey and his staff came out of the tunnel, the fans began to boo like crazy. "Sticks," as we called him, passed Hickey on his way out and the coach yells out, "Hey, Stickles, see how the fans feel about a player not coming out with his team." Coach knew they were not booing Stickles.

After our third loss to Minnesota on September 29th, management fired Coach Hickey, replacing him with our Assistant Coach Jack Christiansen."

The 49ers were Jack Christiansen's first head coaching job. He would remain there until the end of the 1967 season. Jack was drafted 69th out of Colorado State by the Detroit Lions in 1951, building a NFL Hall of Fame career over the next eight seasons and leading the Lions to the NFL Championship in 1952, 1953 and 1957. He retired after the 1958 season. He was named All-Pro six times and was selected to the Pro-Bowl five times, and is a member of the NFL's 1950s All-Decade Team.

After the 49ers, Jack would move on to be an assistant coach under John Ralston at Stanford from 1968 to 1971, becoming head coach in 1972. After compiling a 30 win, 22 loss and 3 tie record he returned to the pros with the Kansas City Chiefs in 1977. The Seattle Seahawks employed him as a defensive back coach from 1978 to 1982. He would retire with the Atlanta Falcons in 1983.

Jack passed away in June of 1986 after battling cancer over the previous two and a half years.

We came back on October 20th at home to win our first game of the season over the Chicago Bears 20 to 14. We lost two in a row to the Rams and Detroit before we won our second game, beating Dallas at home 31 to 24.

After our 48 to 14 loss to the Giants in New York on November 17th, we came home to prepare for our next game in Green Bay the following Sunday. St. Clair and I were on the practice field in Redwood City, on Friday November 22nd, when our equipment manager, Chico Norton, runs out and burns that date into our memories. He told us that JFK had been shot early that afternoon and died in Dallas, Texas. Like everyone else in the nation, we were shocked into silence. St. Clair took the news very hard. He had met the President through a friend, even had coffee with him one afternoon. "It was a very heavy drop," Bob said. "What do you do next?"

Pete Rozelle, the NFL Commissioner, wasn't sure if he should cancel the upcoming games or go on. He finally contacted Pierre Salinger, Kennedy's press secretary, who said he thought that John would have wanted the games to be played. Two days later we lost to the Packers 28 to 14 in a game most of us don't remember much about.

Scoring only 41 offense points over the last three games of the season, we lost to the Rams, Bears and Packers again. Our offense placed last in the League in scoring. Our season was over with a 2 win, 12 loss record; Last place.

After the season, the 49ers and the League lost two legends when both Bob St. Clair and Leo Nomellini retired.

What can you say about a man who stands 6'9", weighs 265, pounds and is half nuts? Bob St. Clair was just that man. There were players in the League that were afraid to play against him each week. Some said he was mean; that's because they didn't know how to handle him. He played ruff and tumble, the way the game is supposed to be played; not like the dance it is today. The man is loyal, honest and a team player. It took far too long for him to be voted into the NFL Hall of Fame. I spoke at his induction ceremony into the Bay Area Sports Hall of Fame and it was an honor. We remain great friends to this day.

The best defensive lineman to ever play the game, Leo Nomellini, the 49ers' first-ever NFL draft pick in 1950, could knock your head off if he wanted to. He was that powerful. He never quit coming at you. He taught me a lot about the game and playing next to him for four years made me look a lot better than I should have at times. He was a gentlemen and, unless in the heat of the game, always had a smile. St. Clair called him a "sleeping giant" who could tear you apart. In some of our games, we would notice Leo wasn't playing as well as usual, kind of like he was sleepwalking. So Bob or I would go up to him and say, "Champ, did you hear what that guy over there said about you and your sister and your mom?" He'd look up and ask, "Really?" He would literally start to fume. On the very next defensive series the groans from the offensive linemen would soon change to moans and become louder every time he hit one of them. It never failed to work.

I don't know if he really believed us or he was saying to himself, "They want to see me do some real damage," and he did. If you took a count, he would have been voted the best liked guy on the team. He never stopped smiling. A Hall of Fame player from the day he walked onto the field and a great friend until he passed.

Nomellini and his children Christmas, 1963

One more story about Nomellini. We all knew he was a gentle giant and the kids loved him. On Halloween he had more candy than anyone else. He held Easter egg hunts at his place and the neighborhood kids were always around. The day after Halloween in '61 or '62, Leo shows up for practice and he's got a black eye. He doesn't look at anyone so I go over and ask, "Champ, what happened?" He gets this look in his eyes and said "Last night I ran out of candy so I locked the place up. About 9:30 I get a knock on the door and there's this little kid standing there, maybe seven or eight years old, and he says, "Trick or Treat." I told him, "I'm sorry but I ran out of candy a little while ago." The little guy says, "Well, I guess you get a trick." I ask him, "What would that be?" And he said, "Bend over and I'll show you." So I bend down, put my hands on my knees, lean forward and the little P---- hits me right between th eyes. I'm so stunned. I damn near fall down! He takes off and I'm right behind him. You know.

You know, the kid could not only punch; he could run, too! After three blocks, I quit. I'll get the little son of a gun next year. After the laughter stopped, we started practice about three minutes late.

We had known all year that Nomellini was going to retire and that the 49ers were going to do something for him. A couple of weeks before our last home game on December 14th against the Packers, Spadia comes up to me and comments that they were going to present him with a new convertible during halftime of that game. Knowing that I sold cars in the off season, he asked if I could get a good deal on a new Lincoln. You bet; anything for The Lion.

I went back to my employer, Walt Jorgensen Ford, and he was delighted to do whatever he could do. We order a brand new Lincoln Mark V convertible. Walt writes out the invoice at dealer cost, no destination charges, no prep charges; adds a hundred and a half to cover the paperwork. I make 50 bucks. There has never been a better car deal unless you steal one.

The car was delivered before the game and presented to a very surprised Leo at halftime before a 60,000 fans, standing ovation. It couldn't have been better! A few days later, Spadia comes up to me and basically says I screwed him on the price of the car. I was furious. I told him if he could have gotten a better deal from any of the many car dealers in the city he wouldn't have come to me. He turns and walks away, never a thanks or even okay. I think he was ticked off that the Morabitos would spend that much money on a player.

In the spring of '64 at the Concord Elks Lodge Third Annual Football Night, the honored guest, Bob St. Clair, was retired. Master of Ceremonies was again Gordy Soltau. Those in attendance: 49ers Jerry Mertens, Ted Connolly, Clyde Conner, John Brodie, Billy Wilson, Matt Hazeltine, Bruce Bosley, J.D. Smith, Bill Johnson, Leo Nomellini, Coach Christiansen and former teammate Ed Henke. Comments from the evening included:

Leo Nomellini, "St. Clair gave Gino Marchetti the roughest time of any player in pro football."

Ed Henke, "St.Clair got the name 'Geek' from eating raw meat."

Matt Hazeltine, "I remember when St. Clair fancied himself as a defensive player and got into an atomic stance. It didn't work so he went back to offense."

I said, "Bob told me he'd teach me everything he knows when I came to the 49ers and it took him all of about two or three minutes." Bob was presented with a new Browning Automatic shotgun and other gifts.

In the off-season, New York sports writer Barry Gottehrer published the book, "Football Stars of 1964." The cover photo shows Charlie Krueger hitting New York Giant quarterback Y. A. Tittle just as he was releasing the ball, with me coming up from behind. The game was played in New York on November 17, 1963. We got clobbered 48 to 14. Frank Gifford called it the best football book of the year.

Now, "class" is a term I use to describe someone who has integrity, strength of character, lives by his word, is confident without airs; in other words an all around good guy.

Every year in February down in Monterey, they have the AT&T Pebble Beach Pro-Am Golf Tournament. Back in the early '60s it was called the Bing Crosby Pro-Am, or just the Crosby Clambake. All the big-time movie stars and pro golfers showed up. Although it was an important tournament to win, it was also one big party.

Arnold Palmer was the reigning "king" of golf and the gallery followed him like a Pied Piper. They were called "Arnie's Army."

Every year, Monty Stickles, John Brodie, Dick Boyd, Billy Breslin, and I, and others from the Niner's and North Beach gang would go down for the weekend and join in the fun. It was either in '63 or '64, all of us were standing on the edge of one of the greens. Palmer was lining up a putt when this little boy runs out of the crowd with a piece of paper. You could hear his mother frantically calling him. Some in the crowd started to laugh but then stopped. You must be quiet when someone is putting. Palmer calmly stepped back, caught the boy, said a few words, signed his paper and gently turned him back to his mother. You could have heard a pin drop. When he turned back and sank his putt, the fans went nuts. I met Arnold a few years later in Concord where he attended a fundraiser. We didn't say much to each other but he was exactly what he showed that day on the golf course, a "man of class."

1964 My Last Healthy Season

We played pre-season games in a lot of non-League cities. The AFL was formed in 1960 and the NFL wanted to extend its presence into other localities throughout the country before that upstart league got its foot in the door and stopped the expansion of the NFL.

We played the Minnesota Vikings in three different cites, Portland 1961 and 1963, Seattle in 1962 and Salt Lake City in 1964. Seattle had landed an NFL team.

Professional football players, if anything, they are eternal optimists. After a disastrous 2 and 12 season we were looking for any ray of sunshine to help us move into the coming campaign. Brodie was back, it was Chistiansen's first full season as head coach and we had drafted this kid out off Texas Tech named Dave Parks.

Coming off a year plagued with injuries, I spent my spring and summer recuperating from surgery on both my knees. The doctors said they were both successful so I received a clean bill of health and I reported to camp with the veterans in late July.

Nancy said I was getting real ornery with all the hospital stays and all the rehabilitation therapy I had to go through, so she was glad I was going to camp.

We lost our season opening game on September 13th at home to Detroit 26 to 17; then came back the next week to beat the Philadelphia Eagles in Philly, 28 to 24. We lost to St. Louis the following week 23 to 13, then jumped up to defeat the Chicago Bears at home October 4th 31 to 21. We thought, "Well, we haven't played really consistent ball yet but we're 2 and 2 so we are in the hunt." Then we hit the skids.

On October 11th we played the Packers tuff at Green Bay in a hard-fought loss 24 to 14. Our defense played pretty good. Chistiansen commented, "Danny handled Forrest Gregg easily, but just too much Jim Taylor." It was rumored that Coach Lombardi stated, "If I had eleven Colchico's, I'd never lose a game." I swear I did not start that rumor, honest. It was well known, though, that the man Lombardi feared most on our team was Charlie Krueger. It was said Lombardi so respected Charlie's ability to defend the run that he never ran a play directly at him. When it came to manhandling someone, Krueger is the best in the League. We came home bruised but felt pretty good. Then the bottom fell out.

In LA the next week, the Rams ran all over us beating us 42 to 14. We were never in the game.

Then back at home on October 25th we were playing the Minnesota Vikings in what would become known as the famed "wrong way run" game. In the third quarter, George Mira completed a pass to Billy Kilmer who fumbles the ball trying for the first down. Minnesota's Jim Marshall picks the ball up and starts running down field right past me standing on the sidelines. Head down he knows he's got a TD except he doesn't know he's running in the wrong direction. We kept yelling, "Run. Run." The Vikings are yelling, "Turn around. Turn around." Sixty-six yards later, he crosses the goal line, throws the ball in the air and starts jumping up and down. Our offensive guard Bruce Bosley pats Marshall on the butt and says, "Thank you. We need two more like that." Marshall had just scored the longest run for a safety in NFL history. Kilmer wanted to get credit for the two points. We lost the game anyway 27 to 22.

Before the season got started, the team formed a players' committee and I was selected as one of the members on that committee. After this loss, I called for a team meeting without the coaches so all of us could talk about what we thought was going wrong and try to figure out how to get a grip on this sled, slow it down and make improvements. Whatever it was we tried to fix didn't work as we lost our next two games to Baltimore and Minnesota again. This was the lowest point of the season.

I called for one more meeting before our next game which was against the Packers at home November 15th. We all sat down at the end of the practice field one afternoon at St. Mary's. I made the comment, "If we beat the Packers this coming Sunday we may be able to 'salvage the season.'" We came out hungry and won the game 24 to 14. Paul Hornung had a partial shoulder separation but Lombardi kept sending him in to kick. Paul missed a couple of field goal attempts and when both teams were coming off the field at the end of the game a reporter called out and asked Paul how he had missed his two field-goal tries. Paul's response was simply, "I can't kick." I picked up on that phrase and have used it all my life.

Hornung was the best short yard runner in the game. When you needed a first down, he got it for you. He could do it all: run, catch, throw, punt, kick off, kick field-goals and PATs. He and I had a few beers together in North Beach over the years. A great guy and one hell of a football player who deserves to be in the NFL Hall of Fame.

In Chicago the next week we lost a close game to the Bears 23 to 21. Then came Baltimore at home on November 29th.

"Walk it off" was a term used for just about any injury suffered on the field during a game back in those days. If it didn't bleed too much or a bone wasn't sticking out somewhere and you could still see, well, with a little smelling salts you were back in the game as soon as you could stand up. A player never laid on the field and waited for a timeout; timeouts were for scoring touchdowns. Sometime during the Baltimore game, their center Jim Parker hit me in the head and knocked me out cold. They said I was out over 60 seconds. No one wanted to touch me. A couple of teammates came over and dragged me off the field. A few minutes later, I was walking on the sideline and was sent back into the contest. I was playing next to Krueger now that Leo had retired. To this day I have no recollection of ever playing that game. According to Charlie he called all the plays and I just reacted. He told me I played a hell of a game. That evening, about 8 o'clock, I'm sitting at Dick Boyd's place Pierre's. I look around and said, "What am I doing here? I should be on the field. We have a game to play." That's how it was in that time. You play or you sit, and if you sat too long you were gone.

Helmets were not only used for protection, they were also used as weapons. We were able to use our helmets back then to make tackles. A perfect tackle was when you put your helmet right in the middle of your opponent's chest just under his chin at the same time lifting their legs and driving him backward into the ground. Helmet-to-helmet contact over the line happened on every play, it was part of the game.

If you had a headache after the game, just put an icepack on it and it would be gone by practice on Tuesday.

An article appeared in the Examiner the following week by Sports Editor Curley Grieve referring to the above incident on the field where he quoted Ray Nitschke of the Packers, "You've got to be tough. You got to prove to somebody you're tough. That's one of the primary precepts of the game, you've gotta be tough. When you knock a rival cold legitimately, you're tough, and if you get conked and can shake it off and return to the wars, you're tough. That's the way the game is played." Ray's comments pretty much summed up the mindset of most players then. I don't know if I'm as tough as Nitschke but I stayed in the game. We lost 14 to 3. If that had happened in today's game, I'd be in the hospital and maybe out of football. I did start questioning the impact of these types of injuries over the rest of my career as you will read a little later on.

We finished off the last two games beating the Rams 28 to 7 and closing out the season in Detroit losing to the Lions 24 to 7; 4 wins, 10 losses, seventh place in the League.

Our defensive line was considered one of the best, as we ranked fourth in the League against the rush. Our line consisted of Clark Miller and me at the end positions and Roland Lakes and Charlie Krueger at the tackle positions. Krueger would be named All-Pro and go to the Pro Bowl for the second time in his career. The first time was in 1960. He was named to these honors one more time in 1970.

We had a new defensive back this year, Ben Scotti, who was traded over to the 49ers by the Philadelphia Eagles. We became friends, and although he retired from football after that season we have stayed in touch ever since. Ben, along with his brother Tony, made quite a name for themselves in the entertainment business producing shows such as Baywatch and recordings with the likes of Weird Al Yankovic. Ben has been very generous with his time and money over the years for causes he believes in. He has never turned down any of my requests.

Our defensive line was backed up by one of the smartest men I ever saw on a football field, Matt Hazeltine. I never saw him make a mistake. Not only was he a big hitter, he was always in the right place.

When he was playing behind our line we knew he could cover some of our mistakes and we played just a little bit looser, a little freelance here and there. Just knowing he was back there made us better. Matt made the Pro Bowl this year as he had done in '62. For some reason we always seemed to be in the hospital at the same time getting worked on for our numerous injuries.

Our offense never really got going this season. Brodie had a good year as his three top receivers, Bernie Casey, Monty Stickles and rookie Dave Parks accounted for most of the offensive yardage. Parks made the Pro Bowl in his first year. J. D. Smith was slowing down. We didn't have an individual rush for more that 300 yards total. The offense ranked 14th out of 14 teams in the league.

Matt died of ALS, "Lou Gehrig's Disease," in January of 1987. His death was the second 49er death from this disease. Former teammate, Gary Lewis, died in December of '86. What made this significant was that Bob Waters, one other teammate, died from the same disease in May of 1989. Matt played from 1955 to 1968; Lewis from 1964 to 1969; and Waters from 1960 to 1964. The odds of three individuals on the same team, at approximately the same time period, coming down with this very rare illness are one in a million. USA TODAY published an article after Matt's death about this strange 49er occurrence in January 1987. Before he died, Waters contacted most of the other 49ers who played and practiced together in the '60s and made us aware of what had happened. No one has ever been able to find a definitive answer to this day. There had been speculation about the fertilizer used on the practice field from 1946 to 1977, a product called Milorganite, which was processed human waste. White things used to pop up through the ground. At first we thought they were mushrooms, but they were condoms. Charlie Krueger brought up the idea that certain drugs may have contributed. Dexedrine was passed out somewhat surreptitiously. I had received over 130 cortisone shots, as did others, and certain steroids were beginning to appear.

In 1987, some early (1960s) team members, Bruce Bosley, Krueger, Waters, Brodie and I tried to have our medical records examined to see if there were any connecting factors that might explain what was taking place. But in a sworn statement by one of the 49er officials in August of 1985, "All the 49er medical records had been stolen from our Redwood City headquarters in February of 1974." We were never told. New research has pointed to traumatic head injuries as a possible cause. We may never know what happened, but that 1964 team has lived under a dark cloud ever since.

During the 1964 season Northern California sportswriters and broadcasters selected the 49er All-Time Football Squad; I was named as one of two defensive ends along with Ed Henke. This is how the team was assembled:

The offensive team:		The defensive team:	
Gordy Soltau	End	Dan Colchico	End
Billy Wilson	End	Ed Henke	End
Alyn Beals	End	Leo Nomellini	Tackle
John Woudenberg	Tackle	John Thomas	Tackle
Bruno Banducci	Guard	Matt Hazeltine	Linebacker
Ted Connolly	Guard	Visco Grgich	Linebacker
Bill Johnson	Center	Hardy Brown	Linebacker
Franki Albert	Quarterback	Norm Standlee	Linebacker
Y. A. Tittle	Quarterback	Rex Berry	D-Back
Hugh McElhenny	Halfback	Abe Woodson	D-back
John Strzykalsi	Halfback	Dave Baker	D-back
Joe Perry	Fullback	Jim Cason	D-back

Someone who should have been on this list is Charlie Krueger.

As usual, after the season the local Fraternal Organizations, Sportsmen Clubs, Benefit Societies and just plain Good Old Boys Groups started their annual honorary functions. These were some of the best times of the year. Good friends, good food, a cocktail or two, great fun in my hometown. I couldn't ask for more.

A 49er Appreciation Day was held at the Pittsburg Golf and Country Club December 15, 1964, honoring 49ers Dave Kopay, John Brodie, Leon Donohue, Mike Magac and Bob St. Clair, chaired by Walt Jorgensen; and Master of Ceremonies, Dick Sanders. In attendance were Bob Fouts, Lon Simmons and Jim O'Neal.

In March of 1965, the Sequoia Club of West Pittsburg held a dinner sponsored by the Pacifica Alumni Club, honoring John Gonzaga and myself. Charlie Zeno of the Daily Transcript was the emcee; committeemen were good friends Eric Romo, Bob McInerney, Dick O'Brien, Pepi Tarango and Jay Jiminez.

I began to emcee a lot of local events in 1961 and one of the events I really liked to do was the annual Tri Club Awards, an organization composed of the Concord Quarterback Club, the Pittsburg Civic Athletic Club, the Antioch Quarterback Club and the Pacifica Alumni Club. Each year they presented awards to the top high school athletes in Contra Costa County. This year's program was held at the Antioch American Legion Hall in May with Tony Knap, Utah State head football coach as guest speaker.

Nancy and I bought our second home in Port Chicago that spring.

Before the '65 season started, Sports Illustrated commented, "If you like the long shots, you might pick the San Francisco 49ers to win the Western Division Title. They have a sound offensive line, a plethora of good running backs and excellent pass catchers. The starting defensive line is deep and strong. Dan Colchico, Charlie Krueger, Roland Lakes and Clark Miller form a young, big and experienced front four. The only soft spot is at defensive end. Should Colchico or Miller go out, Christiansen would have difficulty finding quality substitutes." The Sports Illustrated jinx? I don't know, but that last comment turned out to be prophetic.

Every training camp starts the same way. First the rookies show up, then the veterans a few days to a week later. Sometimes when the veterans come in, some of the hot shot rookies are already gone due to a number of reasons: injuries, the work was too hard or just plan home sick.

The coaches used to think they made the cuts when it came to the players, especially the rookies. Well, we old-timers did a pretty good job ourselves. We would play the lonely card and it worked real well on the kids from back east -- Notre Dame, Ohio State, Oklahoma. We would talk to them, tell them how lonely they must feel not being able to go home to their wives or girlfriends after a hard day's practice like we could. At night we'd hear the cars start up. One year so many guys left camp, management had to go round them up.

1965 The Injury

I heard a pop and went down. I couldn't stand on my left leg. I hopped off the field. Remember, you only call timeouts to score touchdowns. It was in the first quarter of the first League game of the year at Kezar. I was starting my sixth year as a 49er and I had ruptured my Achilles tendon. I didn't want to think of it at the time, but I knew my season was over.

We had acquired John David Crow from the St. Louis Cardinals during the off season. He could hit as hard as anyone in the League, so I felt it was a good move on our part. Brodie was in fine form. Dave Parks had a good pre-season, and Krueger was still on top of his game. We had a fine team going into September. Coach Christiansen said, "If we stay healthy, we can go anywhere."

As a team we had 25 major operations on a number of players over the previous three years. We were literally held together by stitches and scar tissue.

They put Karl Rubke into my slot, a fine player, and we won that first game of the year over the Chicago Bears 52 to 24. Krueger scored the only TD of his career on a six-yard fumble recovery and run.

I was taken to St. Mary's Hospital, San Francisco for my third major operation over the last two years. The doctors repaired the damage, stated that the surgery was successful and I laid in the hospital for over a month.

Laying there, I had lots of time to think about what happened and how I was going to recover from this. What made this injury worse was that at the start of this season, for the first time since high school over ten years ago, I felt no pain in my knees. But I'm young. I figure I have six maybe eight more years of playing time left. Shucks, Marchetti is still playing and he's almost forty. I told Charlie Zeno, "I licked that handicap. I can lick this one, too." At the time, I had no idea that it would take almost three years to come back.

What surprised me was that even though I started the season without a signed contract, the 49ers said they would honor my contract in full and with a pay raise. Most people didn't know that if you started playing in the League season without a contact the 49ers were entitled to dock you 10 percent. I thought this showed class on their part.

I finally got off the crutches around Christmas and promptly took Nancy to dinner at the Concord Inn.

As for the season, we went 7, 6, and 1 tie for fourth place in the League. Brodie had his best year so far leading the offense which placed first in the League in scoring, earning him All-Pro honors and the Eshmont Award. We really only had one bad game that season in Chicago in December when Gale Sayers tied an NFL record scoring six TD's as the Bears beat us 61 to 20.

Six touchdowns had been scored only twice before in a NFL game by one player. The first in November 1929 by Chicago Cardinal back and former Stanford player Ernie Nevers against the Chicago Bears; then in 1951 by Cleveland Brown running back William "Dub" Jones against the same Chicago Bears.

That spring, in June of '66, the Concord Elks Lodge made John Brodie the Guest of Honor at their Fifth Annual 49er Appreciation Night. Over 400 people came, had dinner and listened to present and former 49ers pay tribute to the best quarterback in the League. I was Master of Ceremonies. Comments from the evening:

Matt Hazeltine, "It's been my pleasure to watch John Brodie grow in stature as a quarterback. He's great not only as a player, but as a team leader."

Clark Miller, "I'm not saying this to knock anyone, but the truth is, if Y.A. had stayed with the 49ers instead of going to New York, he would have been second string behind Brodie."

Hugh McElhenny, "I've played with some of the great ones: Albert, Tittle, Unitas, Van Brocklin and others. Mr. B, that's Brodie, belongs up there with the best."

Billy Wilson, "I just want to repeat some of the nice things said about Brodie. He definitely is one of the better quarterbacks in the NFL."

Others in attendance were Monte Stickles, Monte Clark, Bruce Bosley, Billy Kilmer, Dick Voris, Charlie Krueger, Coach Christiansen.

At the end of the evening, Brodie complimented the lodge by thanking Chairmen Don Pacheco, and Gene Keefe stating, "You fellows in Concord have done a wonderful thing for us. This is the finest honor anyone can give a 49er football player in the Bay Area." John was presented with numerous gifts including a portable bar and barbecue, which all of us put to good use.

Earlier in the year in February at Nick's Place in Martinez, I presided over the annual Sports Night benefiting the Martinez Boy's Club. Our guest speaker was the great boxer Archie Moore, who really impressed the kids with his wise words, stressing clean living and becoming useful citizens. When finished, he and the students he brought along to prove his point were given a standing ovation. Archie Moore is a fine gentleman.

1966 Fighting For My Job

On May 1, 1966 I became a free agent. I wanted to sign and play with the 49ers. I had passed all the tests that were ordered by Dr. Sanderson. I had gone to the St. Luke's Medical Center in Sacramento and was hoping that a good report sent by the doctor to our team physician, Dr. Milburn, would help convince the 49ers that I was ready to go. I ran, jumped, cut left and right. In a period of ten minutes, I leg-lifted ten times each 30, 40, 50. 60, 70, 80 and then 90 pounds.

Dr. Sanderson commented, "This man has pretty close to the strongest legs I've ever examined. I put him through 12 simulated plays, cutting, pass rushing and blocking. He passed every test and has amazing strength in his legs. It is utterly astounding considering he has had knee surgery on both legs. The next move is up to the 49ers. They can hire him, release him or trade him. They can't keep him on the injured reserve list any longer. Dan Colchico is ready to play football again. Yes, he sure is."

The report was turned over to General Manager Lou Spadia, who commented, "We appreciate Colchico's desire to return. Nonetheless, Dr. Sanderson is not the 49er team physician. We will be guided solely by the decision of Dr. Milburn."

I gave them five good years. Now, it's "wait and see." I wanted to stay in San Francisco, but if an opportunity came up somewhere else I was ready to go. Remember the 10 percent reduction clause in the contract that they had said they would not rescind while I was in the hospital? Well, I got my 1965 salary without the raise and with the 10 percent taken out.

The team started Karl Rubke in my defensive position after I was hurt and drafted Stan Hindman a defensive lineman out of UCLA in the 1966 spring draft. They wanted to convert him to a defensive end.

Dr. Milburn had not released me yet. I was sitting on the fence. Doc Milburn told me
it might be advisable to sit out the coming season. It didn't look good at all.

The "official announcement" came just before the start of spring training; I would sit out the 1966 season. That was it.

The good news was that I would remain close to the team as I was hired as an assistant public relations man and that would carry me into spring training in the hopes of returning to the field for the '67 season.

Jim A. Norton, out of Washington, would start at the defensive left end position this year over both Karl Rubke and Stan Hindman. So he would be the one I would be shooting at in '67. The team was 6 wins, 6 losses and 2 ties for the season. The offense, with Brodie having a good year, placed sixth in the League in total scoring.

I'm selling cars, speaking at all types of events, talking about the virtues of hard work and the success it will bring you if you never give up.

I really loved talking to the kids. Back then they actually listened. I told them that if you try to improve on all you do every day, then good things will happen. I had a gym set up in my back yard and kids came from all over the place. High school football players would come, lift weights and ask questions. My gym was there for all to use until we had to leave town in 1968.

1967 – My Year of Coaching

Y.A. Tittle
Dick Vories
Billy Wilson
Chico Norton
Bill Johnson

Dan Colchico
Link Kamura
Jack Christiansen

First Row: Left to Right
Sonny Randle, Elmer Collette, Bob Windsor, Kermit Alexander, Matt Hazeltine, Jimmy Johnson, Bob Harrison, Tommy Davis, Wayne Winford, Steve Spurrier
Second Row:
John David Crow, John Brodie, Tom Hoizer, Goose Gonsoulin, Dick Witcher, Ken Willard, Joe Cerne, George Donnelly, Monte Stickles
Third Row:
Dave Wilcox, Len Rohde, Frank Munley, Howard Mudd, Roland Lakes, Clark Miller, Bill Tucker, Doug Cunningham, Chip Myers, Dave Parks, George Mira
Fourth Row:
Don Parker, Charlie Johnson, John Thomas, Bruce Bosley, Dave Parks, Ed Beard, Stan Hindman, Walt Rock, Al Randolph, Charlie Krueger, Gary Lewis.

"He will assume a significant risk of re-injury with permanent disability," team doctor, Lloyd Milburn, stated before the start of the '67 season. At that moment, I was done as an active player. "There is no question that we would have liked to have Dan back to play, but we must consider his welfare and on that basis we could not give him medical clearance" stated Coach Christiansen, which ended all hope; my playing days as a 49er were over.

I didn't like it at all. I had been working out for two years and I thought my chances were good, or maybe I was just hoping my chances were good. I couldn't stand the thought that I was done.

Then with this statement by the coach, "However, we are greatly pleased that we will still be able to use his ability, experience and enthusiasm as a member of the coaching staff," the team announced on February 24th that I had been hired as the defensive line coach. I would assist Coach Dick Voris. This was a totally new position as the 49ers, until now, never had a separate coach for the defensive line. I would be the first. Now this was something I could sink my teeth into, and I made the commitment to both Christiansen and Voris that I would help build a complete top-rated defensive line.

I felt pretty damn good about the prospects of building a strong line as I had what I thought were three of the best front linemen in the League: Charlie Krueger, Roland Lakes and Clark Miller. With Charlie Johnson as backup tackle and Stan Hindman at the other end position, we would be fine.

I started getting razzed right off the bat. Krueger would walk up to me, lower his head and ask, "Can I speak to Coach Colchico?" Clark Miller came up to me and asked, "Coach, what time is curfew?" I had to take it for a few days. It was part of my new job.

The really funny thing was that I was still selling cars before the season started so Krueger and Roland Lakes put in orders for brand new cars at Jefferson Motors. "You got to get on the right side of the coach any way you can," stated Krueger. That was too much, but it did help out my pocket book and they had already made the team so no one got hurt. The thing I needed to do was build a different level of respect from player to coach. One needs to know where to draw the line between the player/coach relationship. I planned to do that with a fair and impartial treatment with all the players.

"Dan looks like he is going to be a natural coach. He has taken right over. The first day he smiled, the second day he tried to grin, and now he can't. We'll be working on our pass rush, and with Dan having been one of the better pass rushers in the past, he will be a great help teaching the younger guys. Everything is a plus for us," Krueger stated.

Our entire offense was back. The League's leading scoring unit the last two years, '65 and '66, was Brodie at QB, Willard and Crow in the backfield, Parks and Stickles at the end positions, and one of the better offensive lines in the game with John Thomas, Howard Mudd, Len

Y. A. Tittle had joined us as a quarterback coach and Billy Wilson, one of the all-time great receivers, was helping him form our receiving crew. Although we lost Kilmer to the New Orleans Saints in the '67 NFL Expansion Draft we picked up this rookie named Steve Spurrier. We looked good on paper.

"I've been playing against the 49ers for 11 years, and this is the most impressive 49er defense I've ever seen," stated Cleveland Brown Coach Paul Wiggin after the 49ers had beaten the Browns at Kezar in an exhibition game on August 14th, 42 to 14.

"It has to be one of the best opening games I can remember," Coach Christiansen commented, "and I give all the credit to my rookie coaches Jim Shofner and Dan Colchico." So the season started out fine, but it was up and down the remaining games as we went 7 and 7 in League play finishing third in the Division and with a defense rated fourteenth overall out of sixteen teams. I was quite proud of our defensive line, though. They led the League in quarterback sacks and gave up the fewest rushing yards.

Then the ax fell just before Christmas when Spadia and his crew fired all the coaches from Christiansen on down. No one was told in person. I heard about the firing on the radio driving home. I'm out of a job again. Dick Nolan was coming in. He had been an assistant defensive coach under Tom Landry with the Dallas Cowboys, so there was no need for me in his plans. I went to the Christmas party in Ghiardelli Square anyway. When I walked into the room, you should have seen the look on Spadia's face. But I had been cleared by the doctors, so now I had two options and I wanted to play again.

1968 - The Big Easy

Even though we had been fired, our contracts did not expire until February 1, 1968, so I couldn't sign with any other team until after this date. Three clubs showed interest in signing me, Atlanta, Dallas and New Orleans. There was even speculation that I might end up in Oakland as a player coach.

While talks were going on between me and these teams, I continued to do the speaking and benefit circuit engagements. I Captained a pro All-Star basketball team in a benefit game for a local girl, 16-month-old Pam Smith, who needed the money to travel to Denver for a possible liver transplant. We were pitted against the Concord Police Department with the proceeds going to little Pam's parents. Tony Freitas and Jack Uddleston headed up the local team while my team consisted of Oakland Raider Bob Svihus, former Raider and now Buffalo Bill quarterback Tom Flores, retired San Francisco Giant Don Landrum and former 49er teammate Charlie Krueger. The game was played in February at the Pete Kramer gym on the grounds of Mt. Diablo High School in Concord. If I recall correctly, we won.

While I was talking to a number of ball clubs about the upcoming '68 season, I found out I had been traded to the New Orleans Saints around the same time as my coaching contract expired. This upset the hell out of me. I considered myself a free agent, as I had played out my option two years earlier and felt the team had no right to trade me to anyone.

Over the next few months there were numerous communications between the Saints and me. We finally sat down in early April and talked specifics. I signed to play in May and although I had been cleared to play by team doctors, it was because of my previous injuries that I signed a "conditional" contract, which I thought was fair in every respect. I didn't know at the time how much I owed my friend Kilmer for this opportunity. He had approached Coach Fears and told him, "We need a player like Colchico. His work ethic makes everyone better." Fears went to management and I was going back to my first love, playing the game of football. I had never quit working out and was looking forward to joining the rookies on July 10th in San Diego to start training camp. I was on to play in front of 80,000 fans on the Saints' home field, the Tulane University Green Wave Stadium.

There was some very important business that I still had to finish. I would be in a battle with the Navy over the next two years and it would keep me in airplanes during most of training camp and the beginning of the season. But first I was off to Southern California. Just before I left for camp, Nancy and I added our fourth son to our family.

Gino, our fourth son, was born just before training camp this year (1968).

Gino with the white blazer, standing with his brothers and their father, in the mid-1980's.

Tom Fears, the Saints' head coach, ran the toughest training camp I've ever been to. I was concerned at first with those two-a-day workouts. He worked us, and it was tough. But my knees held out, and my left ankle didn't bother me at all. I couldn't have been happier. My knees had been a problem throughout my career, and with no pain there and my ankle holding up, I was off to a great start.

Tom Fears was born in Guadalajara, Mexico, to an American father and a Mexican mother. They moved their family to Los Angeles when Tom was six. He was drafted during World War II and spent three years in the service, becoming a fighter pilot but never leaving the States. Tom's father was also in the service and was captured by the Japanese and remained a prisoner until liberated in 1945. Tom spent his last year in Colorado Springs playing service football.

Drafted by the LA Rams in 1945, Tom instead attended UCLA and earned All-American honors over the next two years then debuted as a professional with the Rams in 1948. After being named All-Pro twice and leading the Rams to the NFL Championship in 1951, he was the League's leading receiver his first three years. He retired after the 1956 season. Tom was named to the NFL All-Decade Team for the 1950s. He is also an inductee of the Pro-Football Hall of Fame and the College Football Hall of Fame. He started his coaching career as an assistant under first-year Head Coach Vince Lombardi with the Green Bay

Packers in 1959. He moved on to the LA Rams in 1960-61, back to the Packers from 1962-65, one year with the Atlanta Falcons in 1966, before becoming head coach for the Saints in 1967. He remained there until after the 1970 season. He retired from NFL coaching as offensive coordinator after two years with the Philadelphia Eagles in 1972. After battling Alzheimer's the last few years of his life, he died in January 2000.

Season

The first exhibition game of the season was in Anaheim against the LA Rams in the first week of August. I played two quarters and felt really good. A bunch of my buddies from home came down to see me play. "It was just like old times," stated Mike Szymanski, "He never looked better." The others who came with Mike on this Colchico support trip were: Fatts DeMartini, Syl Garaventa, Don Pacheco, Gene Keefe, Len Gianno, George Grilli and Slats Mazzei. We always stood behind each other pushing forward, never giving up. Even though we lost the game 21 to 17, Coach Fears was pleased with the team's performance and commented that "not once did a Ram back circle Colchico's end. He's still capable of banging heads with the best in the business."

New Orleans Saints 1968

Tom Fears, Head Coach
John Mecom, Owner

Coaches: Billy R Barnes, Ed Biles, Brad Ecklund, Jack Faklund, Don Heinrich, Edward Khayat, Jerry Smith.
F. Row L to R: Charlie Durkee, Tom McNeill, Karl Sweetan, Bo Burris, Billy Kilmer, George Youngblood, John Douglas, Charlie Brown, Dave Whitsell, Eligah Nevett
2nd Row: Gene Howard, Les Kelley, Tom Barrington, Randy Schultz, Tony Lorick, Ted Davis, Don McCall, Steve Stinebreaker, Ernie Wheelwright, Tony Baker
3rd Row: John Gilliam, Elbert Kimbrough, Danny Abramowicz, Jake Wendryhoski, Fred Whittingham, Brian Schweda, Del Williams, Roy Schmidt, Tom Carr, Bill Cody
4th Row: Earl Leggett, Jerry Strum, Mike Tilleman, Mike Rengel, Dave Rowe, Jim Boeke, Doug Atkins, Jerry Jones, Johnny Brewer
Back Row: Dave Parks, Jimmy Hester, Ray Poage, Dan Colchico, Monty Stickles, Dave Szymakowski, Lou Cordileone

Our second pre-season game was in the Astrodome against the Houston Oilers on the synthetic Astroturf August 18th. I was in the starting lineup again and was going in and out of the game for certain defensive positioning. We were well ahead in the game when in the fourth quarter I was chasing the Oiler quarterback Pete Beathard and I went down. At the time I wasn't sure what had happened, but I knew it would not be good.

"I heard a snap," commented defensive Captain Steve Stonebreaker. "At first I thought it was the same one he had broken before. It came as a surprise to find out it was the other one." That's right; it was the other one, my right Achilles tendon. This was a crushing blow. I was out again. To make it worse, we lost 24 to 23.

To the best of my knowledge, the only other player in the history of pro football who had broken both Achilles was my former 49er teammate and friend, Bob St. Clair. He never recovered sufficiently to play the game again. I was really down but I made a commitment to the fans in New Orleans that I would come back.

One of the fun parts this year was when Charlton Heston came to town to produce a movie about pro football. It was first called "The Pro" and later changed to "Number One" when it was released in 1969. The team in the movie was fictional New Orleans Saints. Filming took place during pre-season and regular League play. The real Saints were the background for the movie and some of us got bit parts. I played an assistant coach; even snapped the ball in a couple of plays while Kilmer got the good job of trying to teach Heston how to throw a football. When the ball did leave his hand the right way, most passes went somewhere between 10 and 15 yards. Heston always seemed bigger than life in the movies but he just didn't quite fit into a padded uniform. Local disk jockey and movie extra Bob Walker said, "It hung on him like a cheap suit three sizes too big. Saint teammate, Joe Wendryhoski, who played the team center in the picture called Heston, "A great guy, who, unfortunately, didn't have an athletic bone in his body."

The movie itself was a commercial flop. How many scenes I'm in, I don't know. But it was fun making it and the pay was surprisingly good. One of the producers of the film was new to Hollywood and an old high school teammate of mine, Phil Parslow.

SAINTS FANS!

Let's send Dan Colchico the whole town's "GET WELL" WISHES!

I had never been treated so well in my career as by the fans in New Orleans. I had been in the hospital three times while playing for the 49ers and the fan support was wonderful. In my first hospital stay as a Saint I received more calls, letters and more team front office support than I could ever have imagined. Maybe it was because the Saints were the new kids on the block, I don't know, but I would have given my right arm if I could have completed the season.

Come in and sign the Super-Saint-Size "Get Well" Card at ICB. Just stop in our Downtown Office any day this week from 8 a.m. to 6 p.m. and add your name.
Let's all let Dan know we're rooting for his speedy recovery.

While I was recovering and talking to the Saints' management as to my next move with the team I had time to return to my other job, selling cars and fighting Uncle Sam and the United States Navy.

I had been living in Port Chicago since 1939. My mother grew up there before she moved to Berkeley with my father, returning to Port Chicago when I was two years old. It was my home and I planned on living out my life there. It was a very tight and protective community, a place we should all grow up in.

During the Vietnam War most military ordnance came through the Concord Naval Weapons Station, Port Chicago. The Navy feared another potential disaster like the one during World War II when a fully-loaded munitions ship docked at the Weapons Station and bound for the South Pacific exploded in 1944, killing 320 people and badly damaging Port Chicago. In 1967, the Navy began efforts to buy up the town and relocate its citizens, as I briefly mentioned at the start of this writing.

Public Law 90-110 passed on October 21, 1967 providing $19.5 million dollars for the Navy to buy all 5,021 acres of the town proper. They sent appraisers into town, set up a land office and began negotiations with property owners.

This upset most of the town's residents and we founded a Port Chicago Improvement Association and raised $4,000. I filed suit in U. S. District Court, San Francisco on April 19, 1968 to halt the Navy takeover on constitutional grounds. Named as defendants, were the United States, Defense Secretary Clark Clifford and Secretary of the Navy Paul Ignatius.

Judge William T. Sweigert set a hearing on May 8th on the request for a preliminary injunction against the Navy. My lawyer was John Germino, from Palo Alto. He was very good and he promised to fight with me until the end. It would end up costing me and others quite a lot of money. The payoff from the Navy would average about $3.00 a square foot, but we would push them to the wall for over two years.

Dick Sanders and Jim Scott, law partners at the time, often helped me over the years when I didn't quite understand the legal process in some of my dealings with the 49ers and other business ventures.

I came home to a smaller Port Chicago "population wise" to recover from my injury and plan my next move.

As far as I was concerned, this is the biggest, most rotten military land grab since the Indians. As a citizen, I am going to keep them off my property until they prove to me that the land is legally theirs. No one has talked to me yet. I cannot believe that they can file in court and get the authority to confiscate your land. This is definitely a land grab under the false pretense: It is for your safety. I told this to reporters who showed up at my home after I had run two U. S. Marshals off of my property at rifle point.

The Marshals apparently ignored the sign nailed to Dan's gate posting a warning "No Trespassing. Unauthorized violators will be shot." I told them to get the hell off my property, and they left. I had no idea who they were or what they wanted.

I was home from the hospital and I still had the cast on my right ankle. It was late fall and Port Chicago was becoming a ghost town. Only a few of us were standing fast. We would fight for almost another year. We made written appeals to Governor Ronald Reagan, President Johnson, all of our congressmen and senators. It just wasn't right! I would be the last to go, just before training camp.

While I was still fighting the Navy and recovering from my injury, I had one of my better times that spring of '69 when I emceed the First Annual Fatts DeMartini Golf Tournament on May 19th. Friends were there, including Fatts, Babe Guerisoli, Sid Schwartz, Bill West, Joe Silver, Maury Baker, Gene Keefe, Babe Ferando, Kenny DeMartini, John Costa, Clay Cooper, Evo Geni and Mike Szymanski. Schwartz and Guerisoli won low gross. During the social hour, after the trophies were presented, everyone wished me luck on the upcoming season. Little did any of us know or even think that this would be my last year in pads.

1969 – The End of Football

I signed my contract to play this season for $20,000 with incentives that could bring the total up to $25,000.

I started off injury-free for the first time in the last four years, but I had been relegated to the taxi squad and the specialty teams, kick-offs and punting situations. I thought I was better than the guy ahead of me and to be honest it hurt my pride a little bit. As the season wore on I began to pick up a little more field time, but then I dislocated my elbow and missed three games. This misfortune saved the Saints one of my incentives, so my potential payday would be closer to 20 grand than 25. By the last five games of the season I was back in the starting lineup and on the defensive line most of the time. We lost our first six games but came back to win 5 out of the remaining 8, closing the season at 5 and 9, the best record in the short three-year history of the Saints.

The 49ers came to town for a game with us on November 23rd. Dave Parks and I, and, of course, Billy Kilmer, who was now the Saints' starting quarterback, were all looking forward to the game. Although many on the 49ers were former teammates of mine, I was preparing for the game like I would for any other opponent. I didn't contact any of them.

The night before the game on Saturday, I got a call from the 49er equipment manager, a friend of mine, Chico Norton, who said, "Hey, Danny, did you hear what Brodie did tonight?" - I hadn't. Well, Brodie and a couple of other players were out at this little restaurant when John noticed it getting close to curfew. So he calls a cab and when the cabbie stops in front of his hotel, Brodie asks the driver, "How much?" He said, "$1.50." So John reached into his pocket, handed him two bills, a one dollar bill and a one hundred dollar bill. The cabbie, a little startled, asked, "Tip?" John said, "Oh, sorry," and hands the driver 50 cents more. No one said a word. I thanked Chico for the call and this idea pops into my head. The next morning before we get to the stadium, I send a telegram to Brodie in the 49er locker room which said, "Mr. Brodie, thank you for the generous tip last night but the extra fifty cents was way too much, *"signed, your cab driver."*

Late in the game I'm at my defensive position and just as Brodie sets over the center, I yell out, "John, expensive dinner last night!" He wanted to smile but he couldn't. We beat them 43 to 38. The headline in the paper Monday read, "Ex-49ers Prove Saint Heroes. Kilmer, Colchico and Parks spark win." You use anything you can to win. It was the last time I would play my old team.

I was told by doctors that I was the only pro player at that time to ever come back from operations twice on both Achilles tendons. I was actually in pretty good condition during this season but it was becoming a chore to play. I don't know why -- maybe it was because I was not always in the starting lineup; maybe it was because I had been demoted to the suicide squad for the first time in my career -- but it just wasn't as much fun and the front office wasn't talking to me as they used to.

After five appeals and numerous court appearances over two-plus years, we had lost our home to the Navy. Before training camp started early July, my daughter Mindi was starting high school and my mom had moved in with us in our new place in Concord. Things were changing...

I was standing on the sideline after the last game of the season on December 21st, a 27 to 24 victory at home over the Pittsburgh Steelers. I turned to the other defensive end, Doug Atkins, reached out, shook his hand and said, "It's been an honor and privilege to have played with you this year but this is my last game." His jaw drops and he just stares at me for a moment. Then he said, "Coke, you're only 32; you've got four or five good years left in you." Doug was 39 so he thought I'd be in the League maybe as long as he had been. "No," I said, "it just isn't fun anymore" and I meant it. I walked off the field and out of the locker room for the last time as a player that Sunday afternoon.

After 24 high school, 36 college, 5 semi-pro and 129 professional football games, I was done. You cannot imagine how I felt, both a sense of dread and exhilaration. I had to sit back and plan the future, where to get a job, what kind of job do I want. I had to make up the lost time with my family. As the saying goes, I had more fish to fry. Alaska was coming; there was a liquor store in my future and my family would continue to grow.

I didn't know at the time how much I would miss New Orleans. It's hard to beat a town like San Francisco for entertainment but the French Quarter has no equal. I went into the restaurant-bar business, after moving to New Orleans, with my former 49er and Saints teammates Lou Cordileone and Billy Kilmer, along with local, long-time New Orleans delicatessen owner, Mitch Serio. We named the place The Huddle, located at the corner of Royal and Toulouse Streets. It was a success from day one.

New Orleans is a very old town with a strict historical preservation society, especially down in the French Quarter and Bourbon Street. You can pretty much do what you want to with the decor inside the building but you must retain the historical exterior as is. So while the outside may look a little, let's say, shabby, it's a part of the overall charm of the area.

Getting permits to open a new place there became very difficult. So in keeping within the local culture, we were contacted by a couple of prominent families in town who became supporting benefactors. They installed our cigarette machine and a new jukebox. They even serviced them each week, taking their cut -- I mean their fees -- of 50% from the weekly deposits. We all did very well.

New Orleans is a football town from the little guys to high school, college and the Saints. The Huddle became a hangout not only for the Saints but for most other sports teams. Our theme was sports oriented; our tables were shaped like footballs; our cocktails were heavy. Visiting teams dropped by and we were a regular stop for other saloon and café owners nearby. It was a close-knit, ethnically commingled community that catered to the public, and there are always a couple of streetwise characters who add to the local ambience.

One afternoon a few of us were sitting outside observing the street scene, including my partner Mitch Serio, who also owned a local deli, and Ciro Calico, the man we bought the property from, who was a competitor of Serio in the deli business. Well, across the street, one of the familiar hobos -- I guess they would be called the homeless today -- someone you see most every day, was looking for something to eat. Ciro yells out, "Hey, man, I see you all over town eating out of some of the better dumpsters. Tell me who has the better food, my place or Serio's?" The guy answers back, "Your place, Mr. Ciro. I only eat out of the other place when there's nothing left and I'm starving." Mitch chased him down the street. We didn't see him for a couple of days, but he came back.

Kilmer was well known to all as being a little bit of a carouser. So Saints' owner, John Mecom, Jr., put his foot down and told Bill he would have to sever his ties with us and get out of the bar business. After only six months, Bill was out. As Bill states," Mecom comes to me and comments, 'I don't want my quarterback associated with that type of business.'" I didn't like his decision but he was my boss so I had no choice. Mecom never mentioned anything to me or Cordileone.

"I may not have been a part owner any longer, but he couldn't keep me out of the place." said Billy. "Dan not only made a big impression with the team, the people of the Quarter loved him. If his heart had not been tied to Port Chicago, he would have gone a long way in New Orleans."

I was making good money and having one hell of time but I was out of football and home was calling. So I packed up after a year of being a restaurateur and headed west back to my family and friends.

Mitch Serrio passed away awhile back. In his day, he had been one of the more colorful persons in the Quarter. His nephew Jack carries on the family business. Go see Serio's PO-BOY & Deli, Saint Charles Avenue, New Orleans if you're in town. The food is great.

Sometime between 1998-2001, I got a very nice surprise by my good friend Conrad "Con" Stroer when he came to my home and presented me with The Huddle sign (pictured above) that hung outside our place in New Orleans. "How in the hell did you find this," I asked?

Con's story: "I flew back to New Orleans to see some old friends and remembered the old days when Dan owned *The Huddle*. I make the rounds, ending up at Johnny White's place on Rue Bourbon and ran into one of Dan's bartenders from The Huddle, Bill, who was working there. Some years after *The Huddle* had been sold, White acquired *The Huddle's* collection of autographed NFL team helmets. I asked Bill whatever happened to the Huddle sign? He said, 'Go to Jim Monohan's place, Molly's, on Rue Toulouse. I remember seeing it in the back room there.'

"And sure as hell, there it is in the back room. I thinking this would be a real nice gift for Dan if somehow I could find a way to buy it. So I talk to Jim and after a couple of drinks, I lean over and ask him, 'What would it take for me to get that sign?' Jim just smiled and said, 'Buy the house a round and it's yours.' A great deal. Done.

"I took the sign back to the hotel, wrapped it in a shower curtain and carried it on the plane. A couple of days later I presented it to Dan."

It's been hanging in my garage office ever since. Thank you, Con!

Before we continue on my post-football journey, and as my memory reaches back, I'm going to reflect on some of those individuals who I played with and against; some of the people I met and the friendships developed over those ten years I spent in the National Football League. These are my impressions. Others may disagree but it's my story and I'm sticking to it.

Remembrances

Football is a simple game; it is also a complicated game. The first thing a coach will tell a new player is that football is about blocking, tackling, running and catching. True, but the game is also about concealment, illusion, distraction and deception.

The most important player on the field is the quarterback, period. Everything comes off the QB. Second most important player is the center. He controls the offensive line blocking and must get the ball to the QB perfect every time.

Third most important is the tight end. He can line up in the back field or fight with the tackle. For every yard he splits from the tackle it makes the defense adjust. The tight end can open up or close the field depending on the play called and his set.

The middle linebacker is number four. He calls the defensive audibles that the defense must adjust to as the QB is calling his to change the play on the line of scrimmage. It's the middle linebacker's job to get his on-field defenders in the right spot to stop the play.

The fifth most important person is the man sitting on the bench. When your starter gets hurt, he must come in and play at the same level as the one he replaced. Without a good bench, your team will not go far.

Football is played differently depending on which side of the 50-yard line the offense is on. The offense calls certain set plays to cross the 50 yard line and then certain set plays after crossing the center line. Why? Because you have a shorter field to get into scoring position. The number of yards you need to get into scoring position after you cross the 50-yard line is based upon the leg strength of your kicker.

Players

The hardest hitting running back I faced was John David Crow, St. Louis Cardinals. He came at you with fire in his eyes. His legs never stopped driving; the first hit was like a jolt of electricity. If you didn't hit him right the first time, he was all over you. He came to the 49ers in 1965 and retired in 1968.

Jim Taylor of the Green Bay Packers wasn't that big or that fast; he was just mean. If he broke free on a running play and you happened to be in front of him, he would try to run over you just to let you know he was on the field. Ninety percent of the time he did that.

I was a rookie when Hugh "The King" McElhenny played his last year with the 49ers in 1960. Standing on the sideline, it was a thrill to watch him run. He ran with classic high knee lift and long stride and he was fast. You could see he ran with pure joy. One hell of a nice guy, too.

Jim Brown of the Cleveland Browns was as big as some of the linemen he played against and had sprinter speed. If he wanted to hurt you he could, but he had this ability that when you first made contact with him he would go limp for a split second, which instinctively made the tackler release for that same split second then he gave you that elbow and shoulder and he was gone. He was always the last guy up from the pile when he was tackled. And he always walked back to the huddle, saving strength while building his intensity for the next play. He had 12,312 rushing yards in nine years and was voted the greatest player in the NFL ever. Need I say more?

One more man I cannot leave out, and I use the word "man" in the truest sense, one of the finest gentlemen I've ever known, is Joe "The Jet" Perry." Joe signed in 1947 with the 49ers for half of what the Rams had offered but as he saw it, "Mr. Morabito offered me the best opportunity." He was the first black man to play for the 49ers, was the first runner in the NFL to gain 1,000 yards two years in a row, 1953 and 1954, and when he retired he held the League's rushing record with over 8,000 yards for his career. He was inducted into the NFL Hall of Fame in 1969. He was once asked if he thought he could play in today's game with these bigger, faster players. His response, "If I played today, how many Brinks trucks do you have?"

Very few blacks played for any of the teams back then. The NFL had been the first professional league to integrate in 1920 when Fritz Pollard signed for the Akron Pros and Bobby Marshall signed with the Minneapolis Marines. Between 1933 and 1945, no NFL team carried a black player on its roster. That all changed in 1946 when a number of black athletes began to sign with pro football teams. Woody Strode, who would later become an actor, well-known for his role as a gladiator in the movie Spartacus, had played football at UCLA on the same team as Kenny Washington and Jackie Robinson in 1939. Both he and Washington would sign to play for the Los Angeles Rams in 1946. In 1947, Jackie Robinson finally broke the color barrier in Major League Baseball, signing with the Brooklyn Dodgers.

"I don't think a man's race made any difference to any of us back then," states Bob St. Clair. "They were our teammates, our brothers, and it really never crossed our mind."

"Maybe in the South it did, but we were on the West coast playing football. The guy next to you on the line was there to win the game – period- just like each one of us." he said.

Bob had faced racial discrimination first hand as his undefeated and untied 1951 USF Dons were invited to play in the 1952 New Year's Orange Bowl with the stipulation that they had to leave their two black players in San Francisco. Bob stated, "To the man, we didn't say, 'no,' we said, 'hell, no.'" Those two players were Ollie Matson and Burl Toler both now in the NFL Hall of Fame.

Bob also tells this story about the time the 49ers were flying into Baltimore in the mid-'50s and he was sitting next to Joe Perry. "I was excited because I had never been in Baltimore before, so I tell Joe to meet me in the hotel lobby after we check in so he could show me some of the hotspots in town. Joe leans over and says, 'I won't be going to the hotel with you. I'll be staying in a private home.' It didn't dawn on me until a little later what his statement meant. I remember that when we played in Dallas, the team always stayed at the airport hotels, not the ones downtown." Bob goes on to state, "Dan was great with everyone. Your race didn't mean a thing to him. He treated everybody the same. He is a very good storyteller and he has this way of making everyone feel important. At team banquets or other social events when he was speaking, you felt left out if he wasn't jabbing at you with his tongue-in-cheek and sometimes less-than-flattering comments. When I picked Dan to speak at my Bay Area Hall of Fame ceremony, Lou Spadia tried to warn Dan about which individuals he should leave alone. It was hilarious. Every time, J.D. Smith was in the same room with Danny JD would put his arms over his head trying to hide."

We heard certain words, saw certain gestures, but I firmly believe we had more respect for each other as individuals back in those days than we have as a society today. Too many people are allowing others to shape their lives today. Too many are taking the easy way out demanding that others owe them something simply because of some perceived slight, or because of the color of their skin or their sexual orientation. We have lost the work ethic. You become successful by working harder than the other guy. That is how this country became the land of opportunity. You plant a seed, water it and watch it grow. Eighty years ago men formed teams and started professional football leagues and, from that moment on, also started the ongoing feud between owner and player. I feel a player should receive as much as they are worth. Just because someone looks good on paper does not mean that person deserves anything. That's how it should be in America.

It is hard for the older guys, who have set the foundation for today's success, to understand some of the statements being made by players today, like those who compare the team owner's salary position to modern day slavery. A life built on a weak foundation of "you owe me; I don't have to do it your way; I don't need to practice; and you hurt my feelings" will soon atrophy and collapse. Then that person will not only be living off the work of others, they will also be living at their mercy. Joe Perry signed with the 49ers for half of what the Rams had offered; but as he states, Mr. Morabito offered me the best opportunity. Joe is now in the NFL Hall of Fame.

On quarterbacks, John Brodie should be in the NFL Hall of Fame, but here's the reason he is not. It was because most of the sports writers in the '60s were back East. They wrote about the older, established teams from Chicago, Pittsburgh, Cleveland, New York and in-between. Until 1960, the only two teams on the West coast were the 49ers and the LA Rams. Their teams were formed out of their home cities. They had not migrated from the East like the Giants and Dodgers baseball teams had. Even with the formation of the Oakland Raiders and the Los Angeles Chargers in 1960, they were not in the NFL; they were in the new American Football League and were not taken very seriously, like the other teams in the AFL, until Joe Namath and the New York Jets beat the older established Baltimore Colts 16 to 7 in Super Bowl III in 1969 when the AFL finally merged into the NFL in 1970. Read some of the articles written about the 49ers, the Rams and the new AFL teams back then to see some of the bias and snobbish attitude a lot of those writers took. We just didn't have the talent, according to some, to play on the same level as the "good old boys."

John Brodie retired in 1973 as the third all-time passer up to that time with over 31,000 yards, behind Johnny Unitas, Baltimore Colts, and former 49er, Y.A. Tittle, who went to the New York Giants in 1961 and retired in 1964. John retired ahead of Tittle but behind Unitas in career TD passes. He retired ahead of Tittle but behind Unitas in career pass completions. He led the League in pass completions three times in 1965, 1968 and 1970. He led the League twice in TD passes in 1965 and 1970; led in total passing yardage in 1965 and 1970. John was named the League's MVP in 1970; UPI; NFC Player of the Year in 1970; two-time Pro-Bowl and All-Pro selection in 1965 and 1970. John's Number 12 was retired by the 49ers. Don't get me wrong, Y.A. was great and should be in the Hall of Fame, but I feel if John would have played on any team east of the Mississippi he would be in the Hall of Fame today.

While we're at it, let's talk about the great one - Johnny Unitas. Unitas did for professional football what Arnold did for professional golf in the era of black and white TV in the late 1950s and early 1960s. He became professional football's first matinee idol after forty million viewers watched him and the Baltimore Colts beat the New York Giants 23 to 17 in the first-ever overtime NFL Championship Game, December 28, 1958.

Called the "**Greatest Game Ever Played**," it was tied 17 to 17 at the end of regulation. After a New York punt on the first procession in overtime, Unitas led the Colts on a 13 play, 80 yard scoring drive capped by a one yard plunge by Alan "The Horse" Ameche into the end zone. The effect on the viewing sports fans was immediate. That game, televised around the country, had everyone calling for more. Almost overnight, the major TV networks began to line up games to televise, not just locally, but to as many viewers as possible and the money began to flow as never before. Unitas was on the cover of all the magazines. Bigger stadiums would be built. New leagues would be formed. TV contracts with each of the teams to televise their games changed all the owners' profit lines. Individual contracts would skyrocket. The future would make everyone rich, everyone except for the ones who pioneered this sport called "Professional Football." More on this later. This "Greatest Game" would lead to the development of the ultimate game, the Super Bowl, and 50 years later the exalted stage that professional football is on today.

Unitas was the ultimate competitor. He trotted on to the field head down with a scowl on his face and took over the game. He ran the offense like a field general calling all his own plays. The Colts beat the 49ers seven out of the ten games I played in. If you want to see Unitas today, look at Payton Manning. He's even bigger and hates to lose.

Unitas would remain the premier star in football until the next "centerfold" star came along, Joe Namath.

Joe and the New York Jets would beat the old pro quarterback and the old, established Baltimore Colts in Super Bowl III January 1969 and change the landscape of professional football.

One other old warrior quarterback that was fun to watch and play against was Earl Morrall. In a 21-year career, starting with the 49ers in 1956, with stops at Pittsburgh from 1957 to 1958, on to Detroit from 1958 to 1964, I played against him as a 49er. He went to New York and the Giants in 1965 to 1967, then to his glory days with the Colts in 1968 to 1971 and to the Miami Dolphins in 1972, retiring in 1976. Earl was the starring QB in Super Bowl III, taking over from the injured Unitas. He lost that one to the upstart Jets but would be a big part of the Colts' Super Bowl win in 1971.

In 1972, the Dolphins' undefeated season, in Miami he took over the QB job from injured Bob Griese after game five and led the Dolphins to win Super Bowl VII in January 1973, with one more win in Super Bowl VIII 1974, ending his NFL playing days 3 and 1 in the big one. Very tough - a winner.

"The most underrated player I ever coached," stated Hall of Fame Coach George Allen, "was Billy Kilmer." Born in Topeka, Kansas, and raised in Azusa, California, he would come out of Citrus High School outside of Los Angeles in 1957 as a high school All-American in basketball, All-league in baseball and football. He would receive a $50,000 offer to sign with the Pittsburgh Pirates to play baseball. He received a football scholarship offer from UCLA and at the same time was offered a basketball scholarship at the same school by none other than John Wooden. He made All-American as a running quarterback in his senior year in 1960 and came into professional football as an 11th pick in the first round of the 1961 NFL draft by the San Francisco 49ers. Four years earlier, he had passed up the 50-grand payday. He signed his first contract for $15,000 with the 49ers.

He was inducted into UCLA Athletic Hall of Fame in 2000 and inducted into the College Football Hall of Fame in 2001; Pro-Bowl 1972; All-Pro 1972 and 1975; and Washington Redskins Hall of Fame. He finished his professional career with 20,495 passing yards. "I didn't have style. I just won games," said Billy Kilmer.

Billy and I have been friends now for 50 years. When he came into training camp in '61 we became close, and he would come home with me most every Friday after practice. Then after dinner, he and I would hit some of the local spots in Pittsburg, Concord, the Sacramento Delta or downtown Port Chicago. Mondays was our day off. A few of us, with our families, would head up the Delta to places like Giusti's on the levy behind Walnut Grove. We would water-ski and go swimming. It helped take some of the soreness out.

Owned by Mark and Linda Morais, Giusti's is a fun place and to this day they make the best tripe anywhere. It's not menudo. It has a very Italian flavor. You'll also see many old 49er players' pictures on the wall. Mac's Old House, east of Antioch and home of the $3.50 triple shot cocktail, DeMartini's places, the Hangout and Fatts, The Concord Inn and the old Sage Room in Concord were all stops at one time or another. Every now and then, Billy and I would be accompanied John Mellekas, Charlie Krueger, and others, raising a little hell with the locals. Kilmer got along with everyone and easily blended into the camaraderie of Port Chicago and became a friend of the town. The old-timers still talk about some of our merrier times.

Billy liked to play the ponies and we called him "Tout." J.D. Smith kept calling him "trout," and wondered why we would ask him to handicap a horse every now and then. The next year in training camp, Billy and J.D. were in the huddle and J.D. looks over at Kilmer and says, "Hey, Trout, give me the ball." Kilmer goes, "G__ D____ it, J.D., 'tout,' not 'trout.'" It never happened again.

Kilmer is a giver. He cares for others and it shows. We all have our own crosses to bear and how each of us handles hardship or pain is what makes us who we are.

Ms. Kathie Kilmer and Dad

His daughter Kathie was born with Cerebral Palsy. She has been confined to a wheelchair all her life. She graduated from both high school and junior college. Whenever he could Billy would bring Kathie to any game or event that would be considered safe for her to get around. I saw her many times over the years.

While Kathie was in JC, her father started the Billy Kilmer Invitational Golf Tournament to benefit victims of this debilitating disease. Held in Glendora, California for 19 years, players from all over the country came not only to help show their support financially but to show their respect for the great human being that Bill is.

Bill still continues his charitable work with the annual Ronald McDonald House Golf Tournament in Charlotte, North Carolina, to fight cancer.

Kathie once said to me *"I got my looks from my mother, my heart from my father. If I wasn't in this wheelchair, you couldn't catch me."*

Battlefields

In my 10 years of playing or coaching in the NFL, I found myself standing on some of the most legendary sports fields in the country.

The Los Angeles Coliseum opened June 1923, home of the Rams, and host of the 1932 Olympics. The first time I played there, I couldn't believe the crowd -- 100,000 people.

The House That Ruth Built, Yankee Stadium, was completed in 1923. It was the home of some of the greatest Yankee baseball teams in history; Home of the New York Giants football team, Frank Gifford and the scene of the "Greatest Game Ever Played." The first time I played there I stood on the sideline looking around, "Wow!"

Wrigley Field, Chicago, was built in 1914. It was named later for the Chicago Cubs baseball team owner and chewing gum magnate Bill Wrigley in 1926. It was home for the Chicago Bears from 1921 to 1970. Wrigley Field and the Bears are part of the NFL's legend.

Curly Lambeau Field, 1965, home of the Green Bay Packers. Lambeau founded the Packers in 1919. Both the team and the field have become sports icons. When I played there, it was simply called City Stadium, Green Bay.

I can honestly state, though, that I was never in awe of those or other stadiums we played in. I was so focused on the game that by the time Sunday rolled around I just reacted.

After practice on Tuesday, Wednesday and Thursday, I took the game films home and studied my opponent for the upcoming game. I would watch his every move on every play. By kickoff time, I would be in what they call today "the zone." I never took any man across from me lightly. There were some I could beat almost every time, some I had to work harder on and some who let me know that they were there on every play.

One who always played me hard was Frank Varrichione, offensive tackle, Pittsburgh Steelers 1960 and the LA Rams 1961 to 1964.

Frank was quick and strong and had a way of moving me outside, making it harder to penetrate the backfield. He made the Pro-Bowl five times. Another player was the "Iron Man" Forrest Gregg, Green Bay Packers. We would beat each other up every game. Forrest played right tackle on one of the best offense lines ever to toe the scrimmage line, Jerry Kramer right next to him and Jim Ringo at center. If Frank didn't hit me, one of them did. Then I would look up and here came Jim Taylor or Hornung, with Bart Starr behind. From 1960 to 1964 they stayed together as a team and played football as it was meant to be: hard, rugged and fast. All but Kramer are in the NFL Hall of Fame. Jerry should be.

I studied the other teams' offense and watched very carefully my counterpart defensive ends for anything to help improve my play. Here are the best I saw.

Gino Marchetti, Baltimore Colts, was big, fast, and mean. I would watch him take on two and three offensive linemen and beat them. He got off the snap so fast that he would be in the backfield before most tackles or guards could square on him. The only man I ever saw who could play him heads up and beat him from time to time was Bob St. Clair.

David "Deacon" Jones, LA Rams, was 6' 5" and 250 pounds. He could run the 100 yard dash in 9.7. This meant he could make tackles from sideline to sideline. He invented the head slap; a technique whereby the second the ball is snapped to the quarterback he would reach over and slap the helmet of the offensive lineman giving him that split second to move around the player and into the backfield. I used it many times.

Willie Davis, Green Bay Packers, had cat-like speed, which neutralized most offense linemen. Before defense tackles and QB sacks became official statistics, he is credited with over 100 sacks in his career.

Doug Atkins, my teammate on the Saints, was as big as St.Clair and on the playing level with Marchetti. Doug came out of Tennessee, earned his fame with the Chicago Bears from 1955 to 1966 and retired with the Saints. He was a tremendous athlete known for jumping over offensive linemen and knocking down passes. All are in the NFL Hall of Fame.

Not only did they have great individual talent in common, they also had coaches who knew which talents each player brought to the game. They let their players use their own instincts within the game plan to accomplish their jobs which would hopefully lead to victory.

The thing coaches such as Weeb Ewbank, Baltimore Colts, George Allen, LA Rams, and Vince Lombardi, Green Bay Packers had in common with their players is they are also in the NFL Hall of Fame. Although not in the Hall of Fame, Tom Fears was a very good coach who let his players use their own unique talents within the game plan. Greatness begets greatness.

Coaches

I had three head coaches in the pros. Red Hickey, with the 49ers from 1960 to 1963, was my first. I don't think Hickey knew how to inspire anybody. He knew the game but was such a stickler for detail and routine that it left very little room for the player to improvise as a situation developed in a game. On the line, our feet would have to be exactly six inches from your teammate. He would even come along with a ruler just to make sure. When crossing the line of scrimmage after the snap, you would have to step exactly the same way whether it was a running play or a pass. You would have to turn a certain angle when running down a quarterback. We were all graded on a point system and that was how we were evaluated after the season. At contract time your score could run from 100 percent on down. You got two points for sacking the quarterback, but if you didn't react the way you were told and didn't start out the play as you were taught, they would deduct one point and so on.

Hickey was not a stimulator. He was a degrader and a belittler. His pre-game speeches did little to lift the team into action. Most of us had our own pre-game ritual so his motivational rants went unheard. Red thought that if he degraded your performance in front of the team during a game or at practice, you would be shamed into toeing the line and step up your play. What it did was just the opposite and made most of us lose respect for the man.

Jack Christiansen took over for Hickey after our third loss in a row in 1963. He held the job until he and his entire staff was in December 1967. That ended my only year as a professional defensive coach. Jack did try to bring some togetherness back to the team, to develop a team loyalty, but some of the people he surrounded himself with were simply not that good. One in particular was Dick Voris.

Voris came to the 49ers in 1963 from the Green Bay Packers. I have no idea what the 49ers were thinking when they hired him. He got very little, if any, respect from most of the players. He was a yeller, a sneak and a tattletale like a little boy. His college coaching record should have told Spadia and the others what he was all about. From 1958 to 1960, as head coach at Virginia, he compiled a 1 win, 29 loss record being outscored a total of 1,025 to 272 points. He was thought to be one of the worst coaches in college history. I paid very little attention to him.

Tom Fears, my third and last head coach with the New Orleans Saints, 1968 and 1969, was a players' coach and I consider him the best of the three. He was tough on you, but very fair in his handling of any matter that came up. His practices were rugged and took a lot out of you, but they were tough for a reason, and when you accomplished the stated goal you were done. He never used punishment for a poor game or to discourage a certain player. Tom gave his players room to adjust to the game as it unfolded. If you could beat the guy across from you on your own terms, that was okay with him. Football is a game of running and hitting. A coach is there to teach the basics of the game, to teach the running of plays and defensive positions. A good coach lets the player take that knowledge and mold it into his own style of play. The proof that a combination of teaching and independent play can create victory will show at the end of the game.

Say what you will about recently-passed Al Davis. He knew football. In his heyday, he had a talent for picking players and coaches.

The job of a head coach is to lay out a plan for winning games. It starts with putting the right people together in the positions of responsibility to make that plan work. John Madden fits the model of a head coach. While the head coach has the ultimate authority, a good head coach lets his people do their job. It's the same as a captain of a ship; while he sets the course, he needs the engineman to make that ship move. Madden had one of the best coaches ever in the NFL, Tom Flores. Together they won Super Bowl XI in 1977. Madden had also developed the most important relationship on any football team, that of trust between the head coach and the quarterback. Everything comes off the quarterback. Lombardi had Bart Starr; Madden had Ken Stabler.

When Madden left, who did Al Davis keep? Tom Flores. Flores would win Super Bowl XV in 1981 and Super Bowl XVIII in 1984 with his quarterback, Jim Plunkett. Why aren't these guys in the Hall of Fame?

What do Bill Walsh and Joe Montana have in common? Three Super Bowl rings. Walsh was the perfect delegator. Everyone knew who ran the plan but he let his coaching team do their jobs. And the trust that was built between "General" Walsh and "Performer" Montana has become NFL legend; a winning combination every time.

The 49ers would hire one of my old teammates in early 1976, Monte Clark, as their new head coach. Monte was an over-the-top competitor who came from Miami, where he learned his trade under Don Shula. In his six years at Miami, Clark had built one of the best offensive lines in the NFL. Monte would acquire Jim Plunkett from New England and build one of the better defensive lines in the League and go 8 and 6 that first season.

Then, Ed DeBartolo bought the 49ers in 1977 and made two of his very few mistakes as team owner. He fired Clark and brought in an obnoxious, egomaniac named Joe Thomas as General Manager. The first thing Thomas did was to walk into the team trophy room and start to throw out all the old awards and team history. His motto: "We will make our own history." Thank God for Chico Norton, our equipment manager, who went out and salvaged most of the items from the dumpster and saved them for return at a later date, after Thomas was gone.

Thomas then brought in over-the-hill O.J. Simpson and released Jim Plunkett. The 49ers went 5 and 9 in 1977, then 2 and 14 in 1978. Eddie fired Thomas after the 1978 season, brought in Walsh and put San Francisco on the map.

The smallest man I ever met, not in stature but for lack of personal character, was Lou Spadia. Some think this guy walks on water, but as players we tried to avoid him at all cost. Lou Cordileone stated, "Lou was a mover, a people mover."

Spadia would try to get rid of a player, not only for poor play on the field, which was his job, but also for any perceived insult or disrespect he felt a player showed for him or the owners. He knew the team respected the Morabitos and that bothered him.

Tony Morabito hired Spadia in 1949 where his first job was to be the bed checker before games. Notepad in hand, he would go door to door. This certainly didn't endear him with too many of the players. He would write a player up for just about anything and handed out $50 fines like parking tickets. After he had fined Charlie Krueger and me for missing a flight out of Seattle, he then tried to get us traded for what he considered was a putdown to himself and the coaches.

Krueger and I thought we would have a little fun with our $50 loss, so just before the start of chalk talk that Tuesday I walked into the room with a clock hanging around my neck and Charlie had on one of those felt hats with a clock face. Coach Johnson became so upset he was almost foaming at the mouth. We weren't traded but it cost us another fifty bucks. You could also be fined for missing the team lunch before a game.

Lou was always offering players to organizations who needed an athlete for some fundraising event. It could be after practice on Saturdays, sometimes even after a home game. Most players did this gladly because it promoted the team and it was good for team business. The thing was, it cost us money. The team got the good will; we got the gas bill. We lived all over the Bay Area.

Gas cost much less back then but, remember, our salaries were not what they are today. I sold cars after the season to keep paying the mortgage. So one day I caught Lou in his office and I explained the situation to him and he said, "Okay. We could pay the players' mileage from the stadium to the function." I just turned around and walked out. Cheap is not the right word.

When Victor Morabito died in May of 1964, his wife Jane, and Tony Morabito's widow, Josephine, became majority owners with Lou as General Manager.

Lou traded Y.A. Tittle to the Giants in 1961 for one reason only, to save money. Brodie wasn't making as much as Tittle so Lou thought he'd made a great deal. Boy, would that come back to bite him on the ass a few years later. That trade made both Tittle and Brodie legends, but that wasn't what was on Spadia's mind. All he thought about was the bottom line.

Billy Kilmer commented to me about a conversation he had with Tittle at one of the NFL's All-Star games in the mid-'70s. Paraphrasing Billy, he said that Y. A. told him the best thing that ever happened to him was going to the Giants. Until he landed in New York, he really didn't understand how little the 49er management or coaching staff knew about the game of football. All the teams back east wondered why, with all the talent the 49ers had on those teams in the early and mid-'60s, they never won a championship. He personally believed Spadia looked at players as property to be sold to the highest bidder. If the team won, well, that was good, but that was not Spadia's number one priority.

Charles McCabe, sports writer for the SF Chronicle, even implied as much in an article he wrote back on November 1, 1962, titled "Should San Francisco 49ers Take on Vassar?" We had just lost to the LA Rams 28 to 14 the previous Sunday.

McCabe wrote that the 49ers, "...went on the table last Sunday with the worst Los Angeles Ram team in history and were neatly eviscerated 28 to 14...It's obvious to me that we are saddled with a lingering loser so long as the present owners continue to run things. The present management, in my view, is odious to the point of being inert. They could improve the team, but decline to. They are selling a stale product to a bored audience, with the contempt of a carney hustler. It could not have been said better."

When I arrived in New Orleans in 1968 I was asked the same question: With all that talent, why didn't San Francisco win? The team owned your contract and could do with you as they pleased. In 1967, there were 34 former 49ers on other teams in the NFL. A team needing a player that could help them get into the playoffs would call up and Spadia would write out a price.

Lou held grudges and behind your back would work quietly to find some way to hold you down, as if to say, "I want you to know who has to real power over your career and future recognition." After being named team president in 1966, he fired the entire coaching staff after the '67 season.

While it's obvious that he and I were not close, there were others who didn't get that extra push. He didn't reach out to help many of the old football players. I think it must have really ticked him off when Bob St.Clair was inducted into the NFL Hall of Fame.

Bob is a free spirit. When he played for the 49ers, he didn't pay much attention to Lou. It appeared that Lou held to one of those grudges I mentioned for 27 years, from the year Bob retired in 1963 until the NFL Hall of Fame came knocking in 1990.

The San Francisco Chamber of Commerce, along with Spadia, founded the Bay Area Sports Hall of Fame (BASHOF) in 1979. Why in hell did it take Lou and his crew 27 years to put one of the greatest athletes to ever play in the nine Bay Area counties into the BASHOF? Bob deserved to have been a charter inductee. Simply put, Spadia didn't want St. Clair honored that way. After Bob was honored by the NFL in 1990, Lou needed to save face and bring Bob in the following year, 1991. That's how small a person he was.

Bob's induction into the BASHOF also gave me one of my greatest honors, as Bob asked me to speak at the ceremony. Here is what I said at the induction:

"The first thing I want to say is 'thank you' to my close friend and former teammate for asking me to present him with this well-deserved Bay Area Hall of Fame honor. My routine usually is considered a bit off color but tonight I will eliminate that. There is a time and place for everything.

"I knew about Bob St. Clair many years before we became friends and teammates. I watched him play for the 49ers and there was always something about him that stood out. Not just his size, but an essence that warranted recognition on the field.

"I was drafted by the 49ers as a red shirt in my junior year, and during my senior year at college I was told by Monte Clark that if I wanted to make the 49ers, I should pick out the biggest player on the team. He said if I looked good and could hold my own against one of the best I would have a good chance. So I picked Bob St. Clair. I remember my rookie year in 1960 as being one of the longest training camps and having the sorest body I ever experienced.

"One thing I especially remember about Bob was that once it looked like a guy had a chance to make the team, Bob was there to help. He was a leader on and off the field, including being our hunting guide. During the sixties, I played against some of the great tackles in pro football and one of the toughest was Bob St. Clair. I know because I had to practice against him every day. You had to be tough to play and it certainly wasn't for the money. As St. Clair used to say, 'Our paychecks came with the junk mail.'

"I like to tell this story about Roland Lakes, who was drafted to play Bob's position. Roland didn't have much to say during camp and the exhibition season until he had to go into a game for St. Clair, who had pulled a muscle. After the second offensive series, there was a timeout to carry Roland off the field. He was replaced by the ailing St. Clair. Lakes was on the bench being given smelling salts when Bill Johnson came over and said, 'Welcome to the big leagues. Don't worry, Roland. You just got the wind knocked out of you.' Lakes answered, 'Coach, you should check my pants.' Bob finished that game and the season. Roland went on to be a top defensive player in the NFL.

"Anyone who has risen to the top of their profession, as Bob has, knows it is tough not only to make it, but even tougher to maintain. Bob did it for 12 years. Anyone who was on that journey with Bob (or against him) has respect for him. Sharing five of those years on the same team was a great honor.

"Something that is just as important as Bob's pro football career is his contribution to our youth and other organizations in this area. He rarely refuses an engagement to help any group and especially the kids. Speaking of kids, Bob, at 6' 8", tall must look pretty huge to them. But I've never seen him use his intimidating size as a way to have power over anyone other than on a football field.

"Bob was recently inducted into the National Football Hall of Fame. Joe Perry, Hugh McElhenny, John Henry Johnson and Y. A. Tittle are also in the Hall of Fame. Could the reason an entire backfield made it to the Hall of Fame was because of the contribution a great lineman like Bob St. Clair? I certainly think so. Here we have a person who played high school, college and all his 12 years in pro ball in the San Francisco Bay Area. He truly represents what a Bay Area Hall of Fame inductee should be.

"I would like to introduce 'Mr. Bay Area,' San Francisco's own Bob St. Clair."

A great day for Bob and San Francisco –
A great honor for me!

I always loved playing in Kezar Stadium. It was my home team field. It had all the amenities of a cement wall but it was a fun place to play. The crowd was up close to you. It was never too hot. Late in the game, the ocean breeze would come in from the West, the fog would start to roll in and the seagulls would be landing on the field.

You could hear the fans calling your name. I even got to know some of them as they would be in the same place year after year. When leaving the field, the fans would pour beer on you as you went into the tunnel. Hell, that was okay, but the broken glass from the beer or whiskey bottles shattering on the wire mesh above you could be a little touchy. The really good fans would throw unopened cans of beer. With your helmet on, it was no problem. We would pick them up and drink them in the locker room. I'm not making this up! In a good year, the roar from the fans made you play harder. In a bad year, as Brodie said, "The booing sounded like cattle bawling in a stockyard." I loved the place.

In January of 2001, the City of San Francisco named the playing field at Kezar after its own: The "Bob St. Clair Field." Y.A. Tittle, Joe Perry, Krueger and I were on hand when Bob was presented with a bronze plaque which would be placed on the façade of the stadium.

Our First Reunion to Say Goodbye – A Little Poem That Made Us Cry.

It is 1970 and we've been removed from our beloved town of Port Chicago. We now live in Concord, where we reside today. Nancy, pregnant with our last child, and I put together our first Port Chicago Reunion at Ambrose Park in West Pittsburg. Mabel Tucker and Velda Womach also had a hand in planning the event. It felt good to be among old friends again. We all lost a lot when our hometown died. Nancy said, "I thought the event went very well and we plan on doing it again." To this day, we have a party on the last Saturday in July. Everyone is welcome. Our little group even acquired a sponsor, one of the really great companies I have worked for, the Markstein Beverage Company.

I started working for Walt and Eve Markstein in the '80s, later moving over to Bob and Laura Markstein's business Markstein Sales Company. I promoted their companies and they promoted me. I was working with people who genuinely cared about others. To name a few: Mike Cunningham, Jennifer Grant, Al Markstein, Joe Marin, Tom Smith, Bruce Standridge, Don Touchstone, Vince Vera, Rich Kelly, Gene Visentin and others. The Marksteins and the above individuals have done many wonderful things by supporting local charities and youth programs in Contra Costa County over the years.

In June of 2007, former Port Chicago resident Ken Rand, who lived in town from 1951 to 1964, published the book "Dan Colchico, In Defense of Port Chicago." It tells the story of my town, neighbors, friends and me in our fight to save our homes. It is a very emotional book. It shows how a government agency can tear to town apart piece by piece.

Our great friend and Port Chicago homeboy, Tommy Gott, said it all in this little poem in 1969…

A Little Country Town

Here's a story of a little country town.
On the edge of where the hills come rolling down.
Port Chicago was the name,
Till the Navy played its game.

What a pretty little town it must have been.

The Navy said the people couldn't stay,
That their town was too close to the bay.
But they had to leave their town.
And the Navy tore it down.

What a pretty little town it must have been.

People resided there for years,
Through thick and thin and happiness and tears.
They all had to depart.
But they left behind their heart.

What a pretty little town it must have been

That school and Legion Hall stands there still.
And that little church on the hill.
But there's no children there to teach,
Nor a congregation there to preach.

What a pretty little town it must have been.

Port Chicago is gone forever more.
It will never be the way it was before.
But people who pass through it say,
To people who once knew it,

What a pretty little town it must have been.

Nancy and I would add one more to their family in September of 1970 when daughter Kristen was born. Kristen was an outstanding athlete at Clayton Valley High, excelling at volleyball, softball and soccer before graduating in 1988. She would go on to play professional soccer in Japan in the early '90s, returning to  Clayton Valley to be inducted into their Sports Hall of Fame in October 2010. Six year old Kris is sitting on Dan's lap, surrounded by the entire family in Concord, 1976.

Golf - More Golf and Saving St. Clair

I was playing in a lot of fundraising golf tournaments that spring and summer of 1970. I was still selling cars but I hadn't decided yet what I wanted to do for the long term. My foursomes were usually made up of my buddies who could make it to the course the next day after the party the night before. Denny Coffee, Kenny DeMartini and Carl Jefferson golfed with me a lot over the years, as well as my kid's "uncle" Mike Szymanski, a former Marine during the Korean War era.

John Brodie and I hooked up and played in the Third Annual Daryle Lomonica Golf Tournament in April. John was a great golfer and he won this tournament, shooting a scratch 66. I shot a handicapped 72, and I'm not telling anyone what my handicap was at that time.

John would go on to play on the PGA Senior Circuit from 1981 to 1998, winning the 1991 Security Pacific Senior Classic and earning a total of $735,000 over his playing career. Brodie, a smoker and drinker all his adult life, was struck down by a massive stroke in October of 2000.

We all drank and smoked back then. I smoked for 30 years starting in the fifth grade. Most of us would light up at halftime in the locker room. Back then it was the fashionable thing to do. Some of the better known stars in the League used their fame to supplement their meager season's income by appearing in cigarette ads. Paul Hornung, Green Bay, and, Sam Huff, New York Giants sold Marlboro. Cover Boy Frank Gifford pitched for Lucky Strikes. Even the baseball boys got involved. "Joltin Joe" DiMaggio sold Camels, "The Splendid Splinter" Ted Williams and Stan "The Man" Musial peddled Chesterfields.

We knew it wasn't really good for us but that was a different time. It was our choice. You pay the price of your own decisions. Like the Navy told us that the reason they tore down Port Chicago was for our own safety, now the government is trying to tell us the same thing about cigarettes. Just leave us alone! John survived the hemorrhage and is still recovering to this day.

It was at one of these local golf tournaments, sponsored by the Concord Inn, that I first met Joe DiMaggio in 1970. Joe is another local boy, born in Martinez. His family moved to San Francisco shortly after his birth and it was there that he would grow into his future fame.

I have heard a lot of conflicting stories over the last 40 years about this man, some good, some not so good. All I can say is that he was very friendly and seemed genuinely interested in the conversations we had over the course of our infrequent meetings. Every now and then you could spot him at Vince and Jack Amato's restaurant in Martinez. Joe was a cousin to Vince and Jack, the sons of Pete and Mary Amato, the founders of this popular sports bar and restaurant. Joe was also a snappy dresser.

It was at one of these Concord Inn golf tournaments that Dan first met a young Bill Walsh. Dan is on the left standing next to Frank Enea, owner of the Concord Inn and the theater in downtown Concord. Bill is on the right, next to the smoking man. This photo was taken in 1972 or 1973 before Bill became the Head Coach of the San Francisco 49ers.

If I was not the Master of Ceremonies at most of these celebrity golf tournaments, two of the finest gentlemen I've had the pleasure to meet, because of my affiliation with Bay Area professional sports, would usually step in and share the duties, Lon Simmons and Russ Hodges.

I don't recall either of them saying or writing anything that would have been considered a personal negative remark about a player. If a player was beginning to slow down and began to miss a play here or there, their comments would be along the line of: "He's had a great career but too many injuries or Father Time is beginning to catch up."

Everyone who has played in professional team sports in the Bay Area over the past 50 years has a real respect for each of them.

Like John Wooden's "Pyramid of Life," Russ Hodges had his own "ABCD's formula to success." Whenever he spoke to kids, he would stress these points: A-Ability to be used in the game; B-Brains to learn the game; C-Courage to catch one in the shins and keep playing; D-Desire to play your best and to win; and lastly, it's important not to be an easy loser or a bad loser."

I last spoke to him a few days before his untimely death in April 1971. He was the honored guest speaker at the dedication ceremonies for the new high schools' Concord Athletic League.

Lon Simmons came to the 49ers in 1957 and remained "mister play-by-play" for the next 24 years. He never had a bad word to say about anyone. He had a sincere handshake and was a great storyteller. Simmons was also teamed with Hodges in the San Francisco Giants' broadcasting booth from 1958 until 1973.

When the Giants' new AT&T Stadium was dedicated, the team named the broadcast booth "The Hodges-Simmons Broadcast Center" in 2000.

I first met Ralph McDonald, a very gracious man in the early '70s. Billy Kilmer introduced him to me at a fundraising event in San Jose for abused kids. Ralph was good friends with the Voice of the 49ers, Don Klein and Don Heinrich. Don was instrumental in the trade that sent Tittle to the Giants in 1961. Ralph also became a 49er spotter in 1981.

In the mid-'70s, McDonald started a long running, yearly golf tournament raising money for his favorite cause: abused children. At times I was called on to emcee these events. We played at courses such as Villages in San Jose, Silverado Napa, Peacock Gap San Rafael and Silver Creek San Jose.

At one of these tournaments, we had a Kilmer "roast" at Ricky's Hyatt House. Lon Simmons was supposed to be the host but got sick at the last moment. Monte Stickles stepped up and told Ralph that he and I would handle the mic. I walked up to the podium and asked that the doors be shut and told the reporters to put away their notepads, because what "happens in this room tonight stays in this room." We had all been together the previous two days. I'll leave it up to your own imagination as to what was said that evening.

It was at one of these tournaments at Silver Creek in San Jose in 1984 when Bob St.Clair had a very serious attack of heart failure. I was coming over a hill following Bob's group after teeing off. I saw all these guys standing around and Bob on the ground. No one was doing anything. I ran up, lifted Bob off the ground, and from behind I begin to pump his chest and he began to gasp for breath. According to Bob, I was slapping him around and yelling, "Don't you die on me you SOB." How do you like that! I saved the SOB's life and all he remembers is I'm beating him up.

Bob spent the next eight days in a hospital. I went to see him one evening and he said, "I'm sure glad you didn't give me that mouth-to-mouth stuff." I said, "Yeah, this being San Francisco we'd probably fall in love, our wives would leave us and we would have to move in together."

Bob now lives in Santa Rosa with his wife, Marcia. He and I, along with his friend Mike Venn, played a lot of golf throughout the '80s and '90s at the Northwood Golf Club in Monte Rio. Mike owned a hotel in Monte Rio for a number of years. It was the perfect place to stay and play. Ironically, Monte Rio, which is just down the road from Guerneville, a town with a close relationship with San Francisco, named Bob St.Clair Grand Marshall of one of their Gay Pride parades in the late '80s. *I throw this in here for levity purposes only.*

Rage in the NFL

Steroids and drugs in other forms have been given to athletes from the beginning of competitive sports. Games are played to be won and those playing the games will do just about anything to gain the upper hand in any contest. Sports can and do bring out the best and worst in those who compete to win at any cost.

While with the 49ers, some of us were given Dexedrine, a stimulant, before and during games. We thought little of it. I also had well over 140 shots of Cortisone in many parts of my body to relieve pain, "not to heal," just so I could continue playing for a season. Who knows the total of those shots I had during my career. We never thought of the long-term effects. It wasn't until later that it was determined there can be long-term, even life-threatening, effects from too much use of these drugs. Dyannaball was a new pill making the rounds back then, a steroid that built strength and body mass. That win-at-all-cost mindset did bring out the worst in some. You could take a pill and *bam*, you were bigger, stronger, faster, and unbeatable.

It wasn't until the mid to late '80s that we began to see the terrible consequences these drugs could take on the human body. It hit home in the Bay Area with the death of Oakland Raider Lyle Alzado in 1992 of brain cancer, and John Matuszak of a heart attack in 1989.

Now that we know what these chemicals can do to a person, it would be crazy for anyone to touch this stuff. But there are those who want that moment of glory so bad, who want that high of winning so much, and even knowing what could happen to them, will do it anyway.

Here is my proposal: Let's form a "League of Cheaters." Baseball players who can hit 600- foot homeruns, football players who weigh 400 pounds, track athletes who can run an 8.5 hundred-meter dash, they could only play among themselves and leave us mortals alone. They would have a great fan base. Just look at professional wrestling. The only obligation they would have to abide by is that they must have their own medical plan. I don't want to pay for them as they begin to fall apart. When you play outside the box you are responsible for your own actions. Saying all that, and not knowing back in my playing days what I know now about the damage these drugs do to your body, and if I knew that my opponent was taking something that may help him defeat me, I probably would have taken them and suffered later.

I have been asked many times over the years, Could players in my era compete against today's bigger, faster players? I'll let my friend, Bob St Clair, answer that question: "I wonder if these 'candy asses' today, with their fancy equipment and specialization could have played in our era.

"In my day, there was no such thing as a defensive specialist. We were in on every play when the other team had the ball. We often played between 45 and 80 plays per game. I lost 22 pounds in a game in Chicago where I was a complete mess afterwards. Today they have designated pass rushers, certain situation players, goal line rushers. Hell, I was rushing the quarterback on every down. Some of the players today may get 10, maybe 15, plays a game. In 1963, we had a 42-man team roster with 35 or 36 suited up on game day. Today they have a 53-man roster. At that rate, I'd still be playing today and I'd have killed for the money they make."

I'm all for players making as much as they can, but these players today have become corporations so their investment is in themselves, not in the team. I firmly believe that team and teammate loyalty is becoming a thing of the past. Just listen to some of these high priced whiners, who make 5 to 20 million dollars a year: "I want this and if I don't get it, I'll pout or I'll sit down, or I want to be traded to a winner." This is telling your teammates you think you are better than they are. If players back then would have carried on with these pompous self-shows of ego after every TD we scored, every tackle we made, every quarterback sack we made, we would have been chastised by our own team. Hey, buddy, you are getting paid to do this; it's your job; that's how we win. It's not about you; it's about the team. Max McGee, who scored the first TD in Super Bowl history, turned around, handed the ball to the referee and ran back to the sideline with his head down. His face wasn't showing on his ass.

We played to win. It was a collective effort. We played for each other, not to one up each other. That was how you earned respect from others in the League.

I believe that management in my day held the belief that the players were so hungry to play the game that we would go for just about anything when it came to being paid for our play. Abe Woodson tells the story of when Lou Spadia gave him his new contract. Lou told him, "Don't tell anyone on the team what you're making." Abe responded, "I won't. I'm just as ashamed of it as you are." That's how we all felt. This wasn't New York!

Bob St. Clair was selected All-Pro five times, appeared in nine Pro-Bowls and was inducted into the NFL Hall of Fame. He made $20,000 in his last year of football 1963. Leo Nomellini, ten Pro-Bowls, nine All-Pro selections, NFL Hall of Fame, never made more than $13,000 a year. I made $146,250 for my entire ten-year playing and coaching career in the NFL, and if it hadn't been for John Brodie I wouldn't have made that much.

In 1962, I won the Eshmont Award. I made $12,000 for the season. The following spring, as contract time approached I felt I had a pretty good hand to play so I asked for a contract of $20,000. Coach Hickey, who was now also the General Manager, and Spadia shut the door on me. I waited three weeks and went back with $15,000. The door was still closed. Everybody on the team thought I was crazy -- all except Brodie. Brodie, although our quarterback, hung with the defensive players more than he did with the offense. He kept saying, "You won't get that much but hold to your guns and see what happens." Just before training camp, Spadia called me in and said "$13,350, take it or leave it." I took it. I didn't know at the time but this was more than the old pro, Nomellini, ever made in one season. A few days later, I told Brodie what I signed for. He looked at me and said "That's BS." The next day, Brodie walked into Spadia's office with Hickey present and shut the door. The following week, I received a check in the mail for $1,000. I bought my mother her first color TV, and Nancy a new coat for going out to evening events. With the rest of the money, I took all my hometown buddies out on the town. It was payback time to show how much I appreciated their support.

There is only one John Brodie and I have great respect for that man. The only thing he did wrong when he was playing was to not ask to be traded. Loyalty ran deep between all of us back in the '60s and continues to this day, but the link between the past players and present ones is not close.

I feel that loyalty and team pride began to fall apart as the star system began to take shape in the '70s. TV productions became bigger and longer, and salaries started going through the roof. Today every play is examined like it is heart surgery. Someone scores four TDs in a game and, all of a sudden, he's bigger than the team. Without "him," they can't win, as if the others don't matter. I'd like to see Tom Brady complete a pass without his front line. I'd like to see T.O. catch a pass without Brady throwing to him. The thing that's ironic is that John Brodie had a hand in how all this came about; he was one of the first big names to hold out and get the big money.

In 1966, the AFL started raiding NFL teams, trying to sign big name, unsigned players to huge salaries and long-term contracts. They were doing this hoping to achieve some kind of parity with the older and much more successful NFL League. Brodie had just come off his All-Pro year of 1965 and had asked the 49ers for a raise to $65,000. The 49ers and General Manager Lou Spadia did a lot of head nodding but nothing had been signed by mid-May of '66. Brodie, knowing that there was money to be made, flew to Houston and met with Don Klosterman who was working with the AFL to help sign these players. After a baseball game at the Astrodome and some conversation, Klosterman wrote an offer on a piece of paper. John picked up the paper and it read $750,000 at $75,000 a year for ten years if Brodie would sign a five-year contract with the Houston Oilers.

In a stroke of genius, John put the unsigned paper in his pocket and before accepting the offer called Spadia. John wanted to stay in San Francisco if he could and asked Lou if the 49ers wanted to counter the deal. Spadia said he would call John back in the afternoon of May 30th.

The deadline passed with Brodie unsigned. John then went to Las Vegas, then home and was playing golf with Chronicle columnist Art Rosenbaum when it was announced that the NFL and AFL had merged that afternoon on June $8^{th.}$ "Somebody owes me $750, 000," stated

John and called his brother Bill, an attorney. Then he flew to Hawaii and waited.

John came back to San Francisco on August 3rd and at that time signed the biggest contract in the history of the 49ers and professional team sports for $921,000 over the next 12 years, with $75,000 in attorney's fees. The contract stated he would play for the 49ers for the next five years. He did, and retired as a 49er in 1973. Brodie, a gambler and a very good one, played the perfect hand. What else would you expect from a Stanford grad? When he reported to camp that fall in '66, the players, with very few exceptions, were in complete support of what he had done. We all knew that type of money was not going to come our way but we also knew that he had opened doors that could not be shut again.

We showed him our complete support during practice when center Bruce Bosley snapped him a pineapple, not a football, with a note that read, "One million dollars, less $ 3,000." John said, "It looks like we may have a few parties, at my expense."

More Musings

The first National Football League was founded in 1902 and ceased to exist that same year. The first League director was a man named Dave Berry, owner of the Pittsburgh Stars. It was composed of only three teams, all in Pennsylvania. Some of the players were also professional baseball players. Rube Waddell played football for the Philadelphia Athletics and Christy Mathewson was a fullback for the Pittsburgh Stars. Unable to raise enough money to pay its players, the League collapsed after only a few games. The League's only notable moment in their short history was the first-ever professional football night game that was played that winter of 1902.

Professional football as we know it today started in 1920 as the American Professional Football Association before changing its name to the National Football League in 1922. Individuals seeing the national frenzy over the college game and the type of money being made in professional baseball said, I think the country is ready for one more national pastime.

America was booming. We had just won the War to end all Wars and the stock market crash was 9 years away.

To say the League got off to a less than auspicious start wouldn't give justice to it. It barely got off the ground. . The first NFL star was "The Galloping Ghost" Red Grange. A lot of the country was still playing the European game of Rugby. College football reigned and reporters just didn't get up for local games between the Toledo Maroons and the OoRang Indians whose star player was the "greatest athlete in the world," Jim Thorpe. Then the crash and World War II damn near finished the League off.

But the World War II did one thing; it opened up the country as never before. Men and women who had never left their state or even their hometowns before were uprooted for the needs of the war effort and transported all over the place, and some remained there.

When the war ended, men went back to work as never before. Money was being made and people needed places to spend it. Radio was in almost every home and the national pastime, baseball, is the kind of sport you can "watch" on the radio. You knew the game, knew where every player was placed and followed the pitched ball from the mound to home plate and if it left the park it was a home run. Football is a much more visual game.

There are 22 men on the field at all times and they are constantly changing positions on almost every play. Television is what made the NFL. The NFL was the sport that television needed.

The "ME, ME, ME" NFL

I have mentioned "the Greatest Game Ever Played" and the boom that followed. TV was going to make everyone rich, except the players who started the rush. The NFL has not been too kind to the first players.

The American system of capitalism has always been one of inventors and those who work for the inventors. An entrepreneur creates a product, and then needs others to help produce that product. The developer by his or her vision starts the enterprise and pays for the services of others in the hope to profit from their idea. Therein lies the rub. Who is more important? Is it the idea man or the employee? Neither. They are both equal in their need for each other.

This country used to praise the developers, builders and inventors. Every great product that we use daily and take for granted was thought up by an individual or group of individuals with the altruistic attitude of making a profit from their idea, as it should be. Profit is good for everyone.

The National Football League has always been an invention of dreamers, both the owners and the players. It has always been about profit for both the owners and players. It has become the sport of America. It is "the American dream."

Like so many other enterprises that grow so fast and whose only motive is profit, it is beginning to show signs of bloating and tearing at the seams. Owners cannot keep bleeding the fans with higher ticket prices, outrageous parking fees and ten-dollar beer so they can continue to pay overweight, many uneducated, sometime gangsters, to show off on the playing field, who say, "Look at my wonderful stadium; look at me catch a football."

The 2011 NFL collective bargaining agreement was a public display of men in suits and men in sweats with hats on backward telling the football fans, "Look what we are going to do for you and because you love us so much, you are going to take it!" With some stadiums being nothing more than a rolling gang fight on game days, fewer people are showing up to watch a bunch of egos shaking their butts after every tackle.

I'm glad the professional athlete today is making a living wage. With the average yearly stipend of $1.9 million in football, I just don't know how they can keep a home together. In 1960, there were 13 teams in the NFL with an average roster of 40 players. The average player's salary was between $10,000 and $25,000. Closer to $10,000, but for comparison purposes let's multiply the high end of $25,000 times the number of players in the NFL in 1960, 520 players, and you come up with $13,000,000. This was the total compensation for all the players in the league then. In 2010, seven NFL players were paid more than all the players combined in 1960. This year there will 15. With inflation taken into account, $25,000 in 1960 dollars only equates to $181,951 today. So be it.

There are more corporations playing football on any Sunday in America from September through December than make up the Fortune 500. I'm not talking about the 32 teams in the NFL or their offshoot entities. I'm talking about the players.

The players are making so much money today that most of them have to shelter their incomes or the IRS will end up taking most of it. This is still America and an individual has the freedom to earn as much as they can. But at what cost to the game, to team loyalty, to fan appreciation?

When you see a player today who is supposed to be an integral part of the game sitting on the bench talking on his cell phone, do you believe his concentration is completely in the game? Hell no! His actions speak only for himself. When you see a player signing a football after scoring a touchdown, do you think he's celebrating his team's point? Hell, no! His actions speak only for himself: Look at me, I'm the only player on the field; that's until the next showoff sacks a quarterback, and we get "the dance."

It's all about ME: I'm the guy that people come to see. I'm the guy selling the tickets. What, you want me to come into training camp in condition? My multimillion dollar signing bonus said nothing about that. What incentive is in it for me? If you don't give me the football more, I just won't run as hard on the next play. That attitude would have gotten your ass kicked when players named St. Clair, Nomellini, Sam Huff, Mean Joe Green and coaches like Lombardi and Brown were in the game.

I believe the incentive to win has greatly diminished. So much money is being made today. Why would a player break his butt to receive a championship payday? In the '50s and much of the '60s, we played hard to get to the playoffs because that is where you made extra money. There are exceptions today, of course; you see them on the sideline doing their job without fanfare, keeping their helmet on and running into every play. They are still grabbing for that ring. But most? They get hurt, there goes the gravy train after a ten-year career where you earned $100 million. Who cares?

Most players who created the Golden Goose that is today's game have little respect for those who play and manage the NFL. We have been shut out of most all negotiations on past or even future compensation or benefits for some of the crippling injuries that are beginning to define how we will live out the rest our lives. It's as if we never existed.

Head trauma has become the talk of the League these days as more and more players from the past are beginning to show signs of severe brain damage. Former teammates of mine, Joe Perry and John Henry Johnson just recently passed away from complications of dementia, brought on by years of receiving blows to the head. Our helmets back then were made of a thin hard plastic cover over a $3/8^{th}$ inch foam cushion on the inside and they cracked all the time.

After my knockout against Baltimore in '64, I began to take notice of the effects certain hits had on players. I played in many other games where I don't remember being on the field for periods of time. I saw players walk off the field thinking the game was over after taking a violent blow, then taking a hit of smelling salts and returning to the line.

When the article by Curley Grieve about that '64 incident came out the following week, he compared my KO to that of a boxer in the ring, except a fighter is automatically given a month's rest. Isn't the player just as unconscious as the boxer? Doesn't the player need just as much rest? The concussion must be just as severe. If there's brain damage from the jolt, it must be the same in football as boxing because the end result is the same. But how can you do that with a football player? If every football player knocked out was suspended for a month for medical reasons, professional teams would wind up on the financial rocks. So the solution is simple. Just brush off the rugged athletes, give 'em a drink of water and maybe a pick-me-up pill and send 'em back to the trenches.

Following my KO, I questioned management the following week. They sent me to the team doctor who looked in my eyes, said I was fine and that was that. I did send a letter to the NFL but nothing came of it.

As far back as 1928, the NFL knew about the lasting consequences of repeated blows to the head and helmet. They completely turned a blind eye to this growing problem for years. No one really looked at this and other injuries or tried to resolve some of the safety issues or implement proper medical treatments. It would simply have cost the League, the Players Association and the teams; as Curley implies, "too much money." The denials used by the League and others that there was no definitive connection between repeated blows to the helmet over a period of time and the loss of a players' cognizant physical and mental functions is the same type of denials the tobacco companies used to tell us that there was no connection between inhaling smoke and lung cancer.

I believe the League would still be trying to keep this type is injury under wraps if it had not been for the public becoming aware that NFL Hall of Famer, John Mackey of the Baltimore Colts was suffering from dementia in 2005. Mackey had the stature that made people look at the problem and finally the NFL and Players Association did one of their few good things. They created the "88 Rule" in honor of Mackey's jersey number, which helps pay for some of the families' expenses.

John Mackey is the exception, not the rule. There are far too many older players being turned down for requests or even be listened to. It's getting very discouraging and we are not getting any younger.

Early in 2011, I received a letter from Barbara Harrison, wife of Bob Harrison, a former 49er teammate stating that Bob is in a home suffering from dementia. He can't walk and speaks very little. This issue needs to be addressed soon. Brent Boyd, a former Minnesota Viking and now a player advocate, has been diagnosed with CTE and been denied assistance by the League. He coined the phrase, "Delay, deny, wait until they die."

We don't need the United States Congress getting involved in private enterprise. This great country is already in a mess. If Congress ever gets their hands on the NFL, football will not be the same game in 20 years.

I last played professional football in 1969. Close to half the players in the league at that time are now gone. In 2011, the NFL and the Players Association signed an agreement that will make those connected with the League, players and management alike, very wealthy but they locked the door on those of us remaining, throwing us a morsel of the $600 million Legacy Fund.

I negotiated every one of my contracts. We all came to camp in shape because someone was looking to take our job. Players are being paid so much today and with their no-cut, no-trade contracts, they pretty much can do what they want. Even if a player turns out to be a bust, some teams play them anyway with the hopes of getting some kind return on their money. Just look at the recent Oakland Raiders' quarterback fiasco.

With the new CBA having been signed, players do not have to practice but once a day. They can take themselves out of any game for whatever injury they feel hurts too much. Training used to be set up to get your body into the proper condition to play the game at your highest level. That is what you were being paid to do. Most prize fighters, who try to work themselves into condition during the fight, generally get knocked out. That's what's going to happen to a lot of players in today's game. But that is what they want to do. Do as little as possible for as much reward as they can get.

It's the "all-about-me" league now. The shear arrogance of the players today, shown by their actions on the field and their comments off the field, would make them targets back in the day.

It's all about me, quote: "The owners are trying to get a different percentage and bring in more money. It's modern day slavery, you know. Without 'us' there is no football," this is according to Adrian Peterson, Minnesota Vikings. Here is a man who will earn millions each year he plays in the League hiding behind words trying not to show his personal greed.

It's all about me, quote: "There are some guys out there that have made bad business decisions. They took their pensions early because they never went out and got a job. They've had a couple divorces and they're making payments on this place and that place. And that's why they don't have money. And they're coming to us to basically say, 'Please make up for our bad judgment.' Drew Brees, New Orleans Saints, will make more money playing football than all the players together did back in 1960. Does this sound like a man who cares about anybody but himself?

The only ones being held in slavery today, Mr. Peterson, are the generation of football players who lose more and more mobility each day from the damage done to their bodies playing in the "Greatest Game Ever Played," the generation of football players who played in the first Super Bowl; the generation of football players who laid the foundation upon which the exalted stage of today can be anchored.

Mr. Brees, you should be ashamed of yourself. I hope you never get a divorce. I hope when you turn 60 you won't have to walk with a cane. I hope you never have to sleep in an upright chair connected to an oxygen tank or, heaven forbid, someday have to get a real job. I hope when your day is over you don't limp off the field and be discarded like a broken down race horse. To think you earn all that money playing on the same size field that John Brodie and Billy Kilmer once did. They were men with class. You, Drew, well, just a pain in the a__.

What does it say about a 25-year-old millionaire sitting at a sports card show, charging fans 20 to 50 dollars for a signed photo, as if the

$100 ticket price that fans pay to see you show off is not enough? The thing that is sad is that they are sitting next to the legends that had never before asked to be paid to sign an autograph, but may be doing so now to keep the collectors away.

My former teammate, Charlie Krueger, stated in 1973, after I had been out of football for a few years "The League is strictly a marketing enterprise." That would be fine if all who played the game were included. As players began to achieve more control over their careers and as the money continued to grow, both the League and the players slowly started to eliminate former players' influence.

My friend, Ralph McDonald, who started the golf tournaments for abused children, came to see the change in attitude of the newer players in the late '70s. Ralph said, "I ran a tournament where ten former NFL quarterbacks showed up to support our money raising efforts. They were the older generation player from the '70s and early '80s, namely, Sonny Jorgensen, Charlie Johnson, Joe Capp, John Brodie and Jim Plunkett. They all paid their own way and boarding expenses. When I called some of the players who were actively playing in the '80s or '90s, almost to a man they said the same thing, 'What's in it for me?' One player even had the nerve to walk up to Plunkett and ask him how much he was getting paid to be here. Jim just looked him in the eye and said, 'It's none of your business,' and walked away".

The man who forever changed the way the players and owners would negotiate from the late '70s until his death in August of 2008, was the great Hall of Fame player Gene Upshaw. As Executive Director of the Players Association, he created more wealth for players than any other executive before him, but he seemed to have forgotten those he played with and those who came before him. In response to a request by over 300 former players, including myself, that the Players Association and the NFL address some of our concerns regarding retirement benefits, he firmly stated "The bottom line is, I don't work for them. They don't hire me and they can't fire me. They can complain about me all day long. They can have their opinion but the active players have the vote."

With that one statement he alienated the vast majority of players who played in the '50s, '60s and '70s and we have fought his organization ever since.

It is a disgrace that as of 2006, only 284 players out of some 9,500 retired players have received disability benefits. That year alone, Upshaw earned a combined salary of $6.7 million from the Players Association, and Players, Inc., with a deferred payment to his family after his death of $15 million. It could be said he was only thinking of himself. At that time he became the highest paid union boss in professional sports. That in itself is fine, make as much as you can, but not at a cost to others.

It has always been an adversarial relationship between player and owner. Now it has become an adversarial relationship between player and player. While I would have liked a little more control over my career, I was getting paid a salary to do a job. The owners take all the risk. They put up the money to put the game on in hopes of making a profit. We played for money, but we also played for the love of the game and the guy next to us.

After all that has taken place these past years in professional football, I still love the game. I used to keep in touch with the 49ers as much as possible. I was named Honorary Game Captain for the pre-season game with the Green Bay Packers in 2008, a win of 34 to 6. It just seems the 49ers and the League don't want us around as much as before.

Forrest Gregg made the statement, "We should not be forgotten." Well, it seems we have been.

One last tackle before I move on...

This is one of Dan's favorite pictures from early in his career.

Dan, #86, on the outside with Ed Henke, #75 bringing down Hall of Famer Ollie Mattson, with Charlie Krueger behind Nomellini, #73 in pursuit.

Los Angeles Coliseum, December 4, 1960
49ers-23   Rams-7

Teammates and Friends
Dan Colchico Testimonial 1984

Top Row: J.D. Smith, me, Monte Stickles, Alyn Beals, Bob St. Clair, John Brodie, Eddie Forrest, Lou Cordileone, Walt Markstein
Bottom Row: Bob Titchenal, Ed Henke, Frankie Fanelli, Gordi Soltau, Bruce Bosley
Note: Titchenal was the first 49er center. Alyn Beals scored the first 49er touchdown.

"He, Danny was the greatest competitor I ever knew in football."
Charlie Krueger 49ers 1959-1973

"I've never seen anything like this man's Colchico's determination. He often played with pain, overcame many injuries and gave it more than 100 percent every minute he played."
Monty Stickles 49ers 1960- 1967

"Of all the football players I came in contact with during my career, the one who had the greatest influence on me was the big kid from San Jose State out of Port Chicago 'Colchico'. He knew only one pace and that was full speed ahead."
Bob St. Clair 49ers 1953-1963
NFL Hall of Fame,   1990

"If I was ever in a foxhole, I would want Dan Colchico with me."

       Gizzy Galli. Salmon Fisherman, Skipper

"Danny is a very upfront kind a guy. You do something wrong, he'll tell 'ya. But he would give you the shirt off his back if you were in trouble and needed help. One hell of a tuff guy, not as big as some but a fine ball player who should be in the Bay Area Sports Hall of Fame. In one word, Fantastic."

Lou Cordileone	New York Giants	1960
	San Francisco 49ers	1961
	Los Angeles Rams	1962
	Pittsburgh Steelers	1962-1966
	Orleans Saints	1967-1968

"When I reported to training camp in Moraga my rookie year 1961 the first thing I heard was the great Bob St. Clair yelling, 'G__ D__ it, Dan, slow down.' I looked over and saw St. Clair and this kid wearing Number 86 going at it tooth and nail, without pads. Right then I knew I had to get to know this guy Colchico. Danny's work ethic made everyone better."

Billy Kilmer	San Francisco 49ers	1961-1965
	New Orleans Saints	1967-1970
	Washington Redskins	1971-1978

"He gave me fits every time I played him. Not as big as some but very strong and he was quick as a cat off the ball. If you didn't square on the block, he was around you in an instant. I have great respect for Danny as a football player. One of the best."

        Forrest Gregg   Green Bay Packers   1956-1970
                             Dallas Cowboys   1971
                             NFL Hall of Fame   1977

"Dan Colchico would have played at 50 if transplants and artificial limbs had allowed it."

        Howard "Butchee"   San Francisco 49ers   1964-1969
        Mudd   Chicago Bears   1969-1970

"He was a great player. Dan never quit. A genuine good person. I love him like family."

        John S. Mellekas   Chicago Bears   1956-1961
                                San Francisco 49ers   1962
                                Philadelphia Eagles   1963

"Danny was the greatest. We hooked up right from his first year. I had been with the 49ers since 1957. We both came from small schools. Me from North Carolina and he from San Jose State, not like the boys from Southern Cal or Notre Dame."

        J. D. Smith   San Francisco 49ers   1957-1964
                            Dallas Cowboys   1965-1966

"Dan was a tuff kid, well respected in the League. As far as I'm concerned, Dan was in the top level of defensive players."

        Paul Hornung   Green Bay Packers   1957-1962
                                  NFL Hall of Fame   1986

"I feel one of the reasons for my success at tackle was that every day in practice I had to line up across from Dan who, even in practice, always played at 110 percent. Dan made me a better player and I hope I helped make Dan a better player as well. Dan always played all-out. I can recall every Monday going into the training room and watching the trainer work on him. His body would almost be completely covered with bruises from the game the day before. But he would always be out on the practice field the next day (even after an evening in North Beach at the Red Garter). It was a privilege to have played with him."

        Len Rohde   San Francisco 49ers   1960-1974

"I think Spadia kept Dan out of the Bay Area Sports Hall of Fame simply because he did not like him. Spadia was an arrogant so and so."

"Danny is a kind person, doesn't know the word no, a gracious and good guy. His wife Nancy and the kids are number one. Period!"

        Ralph McDonald   49er Defensive Team   1981
                                    Spotter

"Dan was a great competitor. A wonderful teammate and a good friend. Because of his competitive spirit our team always played better."

Y. A. Tittle	Baltimore Colts (AAFC)	1948-1949
	Baltimore Colts (NFC)	1950
	San Francisco 49ers	1951-1960
	New York Giants	1961-1964
	NFL Hall of Fame	1971

"Tell that guy Danny, I love him."

Abe Woodson	San Francisco 49ers	1958-1964
	St. Louis Cardinals	1965-1966

"Dan Colchico was one of the most respected 49ers of that time."

Jim Otto	Oakland Raiders	1964-1974
	NFL Hall of Fame	1980

"I was working in late July 1960, Danny's rookie season. Dan pulled in front and told me he was off to training camp in Moraga. I asked him what his plan was to make the team. Without batting an eye, he said 'I'm going to find the biggest guy on the team and beat the hell out of him,' and that's how he and Bob St. Clair started their beautiful friendship."

            Larry Reece   Port Chicago Home Boy

L/R – Bruno Banducci, Ted Connolly, Bob St. Clair, Miss California 1964, Sherri Lee Raap, R.C. Owens, and Dan Colchico "supporting" Abe Woodson

Like my father and Leo Nomellini, Banducci was born in Italy, the town of Tassignano. And like my father, he also earned his citizenship papers. Coming out of Stanford, Bruno played for the 49ers from 1946 to 1954, a six-time Pro-Bowl player.

Abe Woodson was the most feared punt and kickoff return specialist of his day. He is third "all-time" behind only Gale Sayers, Chicago Bears and Lynn Chandnios of the Pittsburgh Steelers in average kickoff return yardage: Sayers, 30.56 yards per return; Chandnios, 29.57 per return; Abe 28.69. I made him an honorary Italian, Abe "Woodsonini."

This drawing "Friends and Memories" was done in 1967 by Vallejo's famed caricature artist Dave Beronio. Dave, a sports writer and artist for numerous newspapers in the Bay Area for over 40 years, covered eight Olympic Games, 28 Super Bowls and once sparred with Joe Louis, the "Brown Bomber." What most people don't know is that Dave flew as a Tail-Gunner on a B-17 on 35 missions over Europe during WWII. One hell of a good guy. Never said a bad word about anyone.

Life After Football

I am 32 years old and have been playing competitive football since I was 13. Now I have no more training camps to go to, no more two-a-days and no more one-on-ones. What the hell do I do? Well, like all retirees, go fishing.

Phewing In Alaska

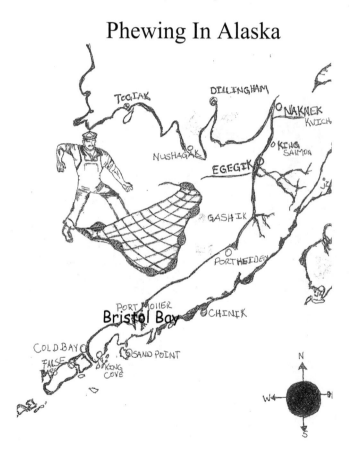

Magnificent cannot describe the stunning beauty of Alaska. The first time I went there it took my breath away. It can be a very difficult place to live in because of the extreme weather changes, but as the locals say, "Once you become accustomed to it, you will never leave." I took in as much as I could but just like football I was there to do a job, which was to catch as many salmon in the time allotted and take the money home.

The fishing business is like playing roulette. Some years you can make a lot of money and some years it costs you a lot of money just to go out and look for fish to catch. I started in 1971, the year after I bought my liquor store. I wasn't sure my legs would hold up, but being on the water didn't bother me as much as I thought it would. At the beginning...

Over the years, I became partners with Victor "Gizzi" Galli, Tom "Guzzy" Rizzo and Savior Papetti. Gizzy owned a liquor store next to Chico Clawson's Silver Knight Saloon on the South side of Railroad Avenue in Pittsburg. When Gizzy sold the place in '76, we teamed up.

We fished on Bristol Bay mostly for Sockeye salmon, known as "Reds" to the locals. We would go up there in early June and stay until July 19th when the season ended, usually four to six weeks, sometimes shorter if the fishing was real good. The first five years I stayed in a little village called Egegik on the eastern shore of Bristol Bay, just above the Egegik River, one of the six rivers that flowed into the Bay in that area. Savior ran the boat and I did the net work. Gizzi ran another boat out of Naknek to the north.

Gizzi's Navy

To say that Egegik was small would be an over statement. Most of the time you would only see people in the morning when everyone went down to the docks to go fishing. The population, maybe 50 to 60, mostly local Indians, the Yupik. It had a city density of less than four people per square miles, and it was home for a few weeks. After a day on the bay, I would be so tired I'd have a few beers and go to sleep.

On the days when the weather wouldn't let us fish, we used the time to repair the boats, and to re-hang and repair nets.

Our boat was 32 feet long and we fished using drifting gill nets. The boat was open from rail to rail and from the bridge to the stern. That open space, "the hole," is where we kept the boxes to place the fish for unloading on the mother ship at the end of the day. We could hold up to 12,000 pounds with a full load.

The mother ship is where most of the boats unloaded their fish to be weighed. The weigher would issue us a receipt for the total weight, then we would take that receipt to the assigned cannery to be paid. There was no state or federal limit on the amount of fish you could catch back in the '70s and early '80s, but there were only so many canning and processing plants so they put a limit on the amount of fish each boat could bring in.

Gill netting is hard, physical work. With a rotating pulley on the stern, we had to pull the nets into the boat to release the fish from the net hand-over-hand, then take the fish out of the net one-by-one. The one thing that kept me going was every time a fish dropped into one of the boxes I saw a lot of silver dollars. I kept this routine up till 1990.

We used a hand hook to remove the fish from the net, then a piece of equipment known as a phew stick to toss the fish into the canvas bags that the mother ship lowered into our boat. They told us how many fish we could load into the sacks.

A phew stick is about 2 to 2½ feet long with a small hook on one end. It made the job of filling the sacks a lot easier. The quicker we unloaded, the faster we were back fishing.

I fished with Savior for the first five years, then moved over to Gizzy's boat in 1976, fishing with Gizzy and another Pittsburg friend, Guzzy Rizzo. It was kind of like a small Italian Navy. When the season ended in Alaska, we would head back to California and work Bodega Bay on the north coast, and the San Francisco Bay when the herring were running. Sometimes I would fish alone out of Fort Bragg on the Mendocino Coast for salmon and pick up a few bucks.

Gizzy's boat was ported in the big city of Naknek on the North Bank of the Naknek River, Northeast from Egegik. There are about eight people per square mile. It would be our home during the season for the next 14 years.

Main Street, Naknek –*I loved the place*!

While in Alaska, I even ran across Jim Otto, former Oakland Raider center during the '60s. There is always a watering hole in Alaska no matter how small the town might be and we found one. We shared a few glasses of whiskey during some of the seasons in the '80s.

Bristol Bay is one of the most beautiful places on the earth, and the Sockeye salmon capital of the world. In better years, as many as 60 million fish are landed. But it can also be a very dangerous place when Mother Nature wants to run wild.

We have probably all seen the TV show Deadliest Catch. We fished some of those same waters. Commercial fishing is rated the most dangerous occupation in the United States with Alaska crab fishing on the top of that list. In the '70s and '80s an average of 37 fishermen would lose their lives each year trying to catch fish to make a living. During one season, eleven boats went down in one day and if it hadn't been for a great skipper and the grace of God, we would have been the twelfth. You always keep an eye on the water. That was the closest we ever came to going down. I'll let Gizzy tell this story.

1980, Gizzy: "Sometimes the day started out clear and sunny, everything looking good. We headed out about 9:00 a.m. this morning. I turned to the east shore and traveled south to the fishing grounds, following my cousin, Sam Liberati. We let out our nets and the fishing was good. Then things got real crazy. Danny was pulling nets and unloading fish. My son Victor had stayed home for this season so Dan was working his butt off.

"To the north I saw clouds coming in and the wind began to pick up, I was not paying too much attention and was helping Dan. In an instant, the winds were blowing 40 to 50 knots and it was getting very dark. Our cannery, the one which paid us, had put on a 6,000-pound limit that day. We were also "princess" fishing for another boat with an additional 6,000 pounds to harvest.

"Things got bad quickly. I yelled at Dan to get the nets in the boat. We caught so many fish so fast that we didn't have time to even out the catch in the hole to make the boat level and stable in the water. We were afloat bow up, aft down with water in the stern gunwale. I thought about cutting the nets loose but Danny yelled, saying they were in the boat. Dan started throwing the fish forward and tried to balance the boat as I started for home.

"I knew if I turned straight back to the river and toward the mother ship, it would be too far to go in this wind out of the southeast. So I headed for the beach across the bay, protected by some high bluffs, and tried to get out of the wind, now up to 80 knots. Our radio antenna had blown down so while I could hear others calling us, I could not call back. We were on our own.

"Nearing the shore, Dan threw the anchor onto the beach in shallow water. It held and we started moving the fish around. This was very dangerous because the tides turn very quickly up there, dropping as much as 23 feet. If that had happened, it would have been all over. We fought a hell of a battle and were losing. Finally, the fish were spread properly. Then I turned the key and the engine wouldn't start. I made the sign of the cross and thanked God that my son Victor had not come up for this season. That's the most scared I've ever been. I looked at Dan; he looked at me...

"Then the miracle happened. My uncle, Sam Papetti, who had also been fishing that day reached me on the radio and turned his boat around, hooked us up and pulled us to the mother ship for unloading. But our trials were not over just yet. The weather wasn't any better there than out in the bay but the ships were bigger and they blocked the wind a little. Danny threw the line up to the deckhand who tied it off and we got ready to toss in the fish, but we broke loose and started drifting into the middle of all these ships. This time it was my cousin who was standing by and he towed us back to the mother ship. Dan threw the line up and yelled, 'If we break loose again, I'm going to break your neck.'

"Just as Dan and I began to load the fish into the sacks, the mother ship slipped her anchor and began to drift, with us attached, right into the middle of another ship. Well, this was too much. It was against all odds that we didn't drown, but now we were going to be crushed to death. The mother ship grabbed and the nightmare was over. I received two receipts - one for 6,000 pounds that day and for 6,000 pounds the next day. One of the tender boats pulled us up the river and to the bunkhouse. Home at last.

"Danny was the best hand I ever had. He never quit. That's one of the reasons we made it that day. He even fished one season with broken ribs and never said a word. Some years we made big money; some years we made a little money. We always made some money. We were the top boat in the fleet in Danny's first year with me in 1976.

Boatload of "Alaska Gold" – Pink Salmon

Gizzy and son Victor and Dan, Bunkhouse Naknek

"Dan's son Joseph fished with me in 1996. Like his dad, he was big and strong. Dan's youngest son Gino also fished in Alaska with the Grossi's, who used set-netting."

One year, Gizzy and I were fishing off the coast of Bodega Bay for salmon and I wasn't paying attention to the water like I should have been. I looked over to my right, the ocean side, and all I saw was water. I turned to my left, the shore side, and all I saw was water. We had drifted into a 30-foot swell of water. I yelled, "We got to get the hell out of here," and Gizzy managed to maneuver us over the top of the incoming wave. That was the closest to ever going down outside of Alaska. Gizzy is as good a captain as anyone who fished those years.

The year I quit fishing was 1990. That fall, the City of Pittsburg unveiled a seven-foot bronze statue called the "Pioneer Fisherman." It had been in the planning stages for a number of years by local artist and fisherman, Frank J. Vitalie. The statue was dedicated to Frank's father John, a fisherman out of Collinsville, and to all the Italian settlers who fished the Sacramento River Delta for their livelihood in the early and mid 20th Century.

I was 53 years old and Italian, in fairly good shape and had fished for a living; perfect for the job as a model for this historical image. I was honored to be a part of this area's heritage. When you walk downtown Pittsburg, there I am, all seven feet of me -- well, not all of me. Frank used my shoulders, arms and hands. Hell, I wish I looked like that today.

In 1970, the year before I started fishing, Nancy and I opened Colchico Liquors at the corner of Oak Grove Road and Monument Boulevard. It was called Four Corners in Concord, across the street from the Corner Club and ¼ Pound Burgers. Nancy ran the business when I was gone and our older kids, Mindi, Joseph, Dominic and even Matthew after he turned ten, worked there during summer break. In those days, children underage could work around liquor as long as their parents owned the store.

I quickly discovered that standing on a concert floor all day wasn't good for my legs. Fishing wasn't that good either but at least I could get off my feet at times. We were making good money until Fair Trade came in and started siphoning off our profits in the name of equality. It has always been the same; when a government bureaucracy mandates regulation in the name of fairness, the inevitable outcome is that everyone becomes poorer. In the late 1970s, the neighborhood began to go downhill. Nancy began to feel a little uncomfortable after we had been burglarized a couple of times, so we packed up and sold the place in 1980.

A favorite memory of mine happened in June of 1999. Nancy and I went to New York to watch our daughter Kristen receive her doctorate from Columbia University. We stayed in a hotel near Central Park and I sought out a small, local bar as my watering hole. It was there that I met Corky Ramirez, a stage manager for the theater where David Letterman appeared nightly to do his show. I told Corky that we had tickets for that evening and he said, "I will take care of you." He arranged to have Nancy's sister Marjorie, who had accompanied us on the trip, and me sit up front on the aisle. He told us that if Letterman stepped into the audience and stood near us to stand up and engage him. He said that I should not try to tell Letterman any jokes as he was the comedian. We ended up having a conversation for a few minutes and then it was over. During the commercial break, I made one of my dollar rings and sent it backstage to Letterman. When he came out again, he acknowledged receiving the ring, then went on to interview his guests, Helen Hunt and Courtney Love who, when they saw the ring, wanted one, too. So I made two more rings and sent them backstage at the next commercial break. At the end of the show, Letterman said, "We have a gift for Dan," and presented me with one of his ties covered in dollar bills.

The Colchico Ring

The Letterman Tie

Back to Football for a Good Cause

I stayed in touch with Jim Otto through our playing days in the '60s, in Alaska in the '80s and at events over the years. When Jim called and asked me to help kick off a business venture that could help out former retired NFL players, I said, "Absolutely."

In the spring of 2000, Oakland Raider Jim Otto and Alameda artist Gil Garitano formed a corporation called Sport Legends Group, Inc. The name of the venture was called the Hall Of Fame Series, Sport Legends. It was to be a line of handcrafted lager beers and specialty wines that would be packaged in cans and bottles with painted portrait labels of professional football players.

I thought it was a hell of an idea. Beer and football, the right combination. Bob St. Clair, R. C. Owens and I represented the 49ers; Daryle Lamonica, Raymond Chester, Marv Hubbard and Jim Otto, the Raiders. Other players were Tony Dorsett, Dallas; Jack Ham, Pittsburgh; Fuzzy Thurston, Green Bay; Gayle Sayers, Chicago; Ron Jaworski and Lance Alworth, San Diego; Emerson Boozer, NY Jets; Jim Marshall, Minnesota; Paul Warfield, Miami; and Y.A. Tittle, NY Giants.

The premise behind this corporation was to create a Dire Need Fund out of the profits from the sale of our products. The monies would then be funneled to those former players in dire financial and medical need.

Jim's idea was to go to all the cities that were home to an NFL team, find a local brewery and explain to them what we wanted to do. The brewery could make a profit and the money we made would go to help retired players from that city's team. Most went along with the idea.

We had the press conference, got the fanfare going, produced product samples and even sold a couple of cases to a few Costco stores. Then we ran into some NFL copyright infringements. We were working on fixing those problems when Jim became gravely ill. All the injuries that he had endured through his playing days finally caught up to him. He was incapacitated for a very long time. So without him, the company slowly died. I don't recall if we ever made any money but the idea was a good one and the need still exists today. I've got a few six packs laying around. Maybe I should send them to the NFL Hall of Fame.

Lou Spadia did one thing that honored some of the former 49er players. He created the All-Italian 49er team in 1981.

Offense Team:		**Defense Team:**	
Mike Bettiga	End	Dan Colchico	Defense End
Paul Salata	End	Ed Balatti	Defense End
Leo Nomellini	Tackle	Leo Nomellini	Tackle
Don Campora	Tackle	Al Carapella	Tackle
Bruno Banducci	Guard	Frank Casara	Line Backer
Lou Palatella	Guard	Tony Sardisco	Line Backer
Tino Sabuco	Center	Gordy Ceresino	Line Backer
Pete Franceschi	Half-Back	Ken Casanega	Defense Back
Jim Mona	Half-Back	Bobby Luna	Defense Back
Len Masini	Full-Back	Ben Scotti	Defense Back
Joe Montana	Quarter-Back	Tony Teresa	Defense Back

I was inducted into the Chicago National Italian American Sports Hall of Fame in 1980, a great honor as an athlete.

Wrapping It Up

As the saying goes, life is what you make of it. These last 40-plus years since I suited up every Sunday in the fall have been one wonderful adventure. Most of the time, it has been more challenging than trying to beat up the guy across from me.

You have to work and work hard when you have a family to take care of. Your reward for that work will show every day as you watch your kids grow into adulthood.

Nancy raised our children with the care and discipline that only a mother can give and it made me realize that she is as tough as any man I ever faced.

Being gone as much as I was, making a living from football, fishing and all the rest, made her the rock of the family. I know it, and so do the kids.

I've been blessed that the family is all together again. Mindi returned to us in early 2009. It was as if she and her mother were never apart, although I must admit it took time for me to come around. But she is my daughter and I love her, as I do all of my children.

The holidays are filled with good times and laughter as the family comes together to share their lives and catch up with all that is new. As the adults gather around the table, you can hear the patter of little (and not so little) feet running all over the place.

Our first granddaughter Rochelle was born in 1985, followed by Daniel, Talia, Zachariah, Cecelia, Kyleigh Jai, Maxx, Nico, Sonny, Juliannah, and Leo in 2007. Great grandchildren to follow…

Someone once said, "Happiness in not perfect until it is shared," and we do our best to share that happiness.

The Colchico "Team"

FINAL... FINAL... FINAL

Over half of my 49er teammates from the 1960 season are gone, and with each passing day more of my hometown boys pass on as well, and that's how it is. I want to thank each of them for traveling the journey with me.

"I sure had some good times. I want a few more, of course, but man, what a blast it's been. Football is a great game even though I've broken all my fingers, dislocated both shoulders and my left elbow, had both knees operated on a total of seven times, as well as four Achilles tendon operations. My hands, knees and back are so screwed up with arthritis I can't sit or stand for too long and closing my hand is a chore. Ah, what the hell. I can't kick."

To sum it all up, I was sitting in Dan's garage one afternoon talking to him about the book and his past. He said, "Football saved me. If it hadn't been for the game and being able to work out my urge to be physical, I guess there is no telling how I might have ended up. Football gave me the discipline. Nancy made me responsible. Everything followed after that.

When asked if he would do it all over again?

"Sure. What else can you do on a Sunday afternoon? You can't spend all day in church."

Dan Colchico

The Pride of Port Chicago
Dan Colchico

INDEX

Aguilar, Lou	8
Albert, Frankie	46, 47
Allen, George	120, 125
Alworth, Lance	173
Alzado, Lyle	141
Amato, Pete & Mary	138
Amato, Vince & Jack	138
Ameche, Alan "The Horse"	119
Areniver, Joe	58
Arnett, Jon	69, 73
Arnold, Sam	8, 22
Atkins, Doug	102, 109, 124
Baker, Dave	53, 58, 89
Baker, Maury	106
Bates, Jim	8, 15, 16, 22, 28
Beals, Alyn	46, 70, 89, 157
Beronio, Dave	8, 163
Berry, Dave	146
Bessiere, Maurice	63
Bethard, Pete	102
Blanchard, 'Doc' (Mr. Inside)	46
Boozer, Emerson	173
Boschetti, Hug	33, 35
Bosley, Bruce	70, 76, 82
Boyd, Brent	152

Boyd, Dick	8, 42, 63, 65, 83, 86
Boyer, Herv "Hubie"	36
Bratkowski, Zeke	75
Breedlove, Rod	50
Brees, Drew	153
Breslin, Billy	83
Brodie, John	7, 56, 59, 63, 64, 68, 69, 70, 72, 75, 76, 82, 83, 84, 88, 89, 91, 92, 93, 95, 96, 108, 109, 117, 118, 129, 133, 137, 143, 144, 145, 153, 154, 157
Brown, Cotton	20
Brown, Jim	58, 69, 73, 74, 115
Brown, Rocky	54
Buffa, Hal	33
Burke, Don	70
Caen, Herb	63
Calico, Ciro	111
Capp, Joe	63, 154
Capraole, Joe	63
Casey, Bernie	87
Caudell, Earl	61
CC Riders	28, 39, 41
Chamberlain, Wilt	66
Chester, Raymond	173
Christiansen, Coach Jack	82, 85, 88, 93, 96, 145, 157
Clark, Monte	51, 54, 55, 61, 70, 93, 127, 131
Clifford, Clark	105
Coffee, Dennis	8, 38, 40, 41, 137
Colchico, Cecelia Susan	13, 14
Colchico, Mario Giuseppe (Joe)	13, 14, 16
Conner, Clyde	68, 82
Connolly, Ted	53, 70, 82, 89, 162
Cooper, Clay	106
Cordileone, Lou	7, 59, 102, 110, 128, 175, 158
Costa, John	106

Name	Pages
Couchman, Jim	8
Crow, John David	74, 91, 96, 97, 115
Cunningham, Mike	134
Davis, Al	126, 127
Davis, Glen (Mr. Outside)	46
Davis, Willie	124
DeBartolo, Eddie	127
Delaganese, Frank	62
DeMarco, Bino	20
DeMarco, Leo	20
DeMartini, Fatts	8, 70, 101, 106, 121
DeMartini, Kenny	8, 106, 137
DeRosa, Don	70
Donohue, Leon	89
Dorsett, Tony	173
Dove, Eddie	51, 61
Dowler, Boyd	65
Duncan, Mark	50
Earl, Ron	38
Easter, Curtis	8, 15, 16, 22
Edleman,, Bill	26
Elliason, Jim	61
Enea, Frank	138
Eshmont, Len	12, 74, 76, 92, 143
Ewbank, Weeb	125
Fairclough, Hart	30
Fears, Coach Tom	99, 100, 101, 102, 125, 126,
Feldman, Coach Marty	45
Ferrando, Babe	106
Flores, Tom	99, 127
Forrest, Eddie	70, 159
Fouts, Bob	89
Franz, Rod	26, 27, 28, 32, 61
Freitas, Tony	99
Fugler, Max	54
Gagne, Verne	54

Galli, Gizzi	8, 165, 166
Gandera, Walter	61
Garaventa, Sil	101
Garitano, Gil	173
Gaunt, Stan	8, 28, 29
Gehrig, Lou	88
Germino, John	105
Gianno, Len	101
Gifford, Frank	83, 123, 137
Gini, Evo	106
Gomes, Eddie	70
Gonzaga, John	7, 21, 48, 60, 78, 89
Gott, Tommy	8, 22, 135
Gottehrer, Barry	82
Graham, Otto	46
Grange, Red "The Galloping Ghost"	146
Grant, Jennifer	134
Green, 'Mean Joe'	150
Gregg, Forrest	7, 57, 58, 84, 124, 155, 159
Griese, Bob	120
Grieve, Curley	87, 150
Grilli, George	61, 101
Grossi, Americo "Firpo"	21, 22
Grossi, Dave	21
Guerisoli, Babe	106, 107
Ham, Jack	173
Hangerty, Walt & Ruth	60
Harrison, Bob (Hog)	51, 54, 96, 152
Hazeltine, Matt	50, 51, 58, 64, 72, 73, 76, 82, 87, 89, 92, 96
Heinrich, Don	102, 139
Henke, Ed	52, 53, 54, 59, 70, 82, 89, 156, 157
Heston, Charlton	103
Hickey, Coach "Red"	48, 50, 51, 55, 56, 58, 67, 69, 77, 78, 125, 126, 143
Hindman, Stan	94, 95, 96, 97
Hodges, Russ	138, 139

Hombre, Montana	54
Hornung, Paul	7, 59, 65, 73, 85, 86, 124, 134, 160
Hrubi, Dan	61
Hubbard, Marv	173
Huff, Sam	137
Ignatius, Paul	105
Jacobsen, Ralph	22
Jaworski, Ron	173
Jiminez, Jay	90
Johnson Hugh	22
Johnson, Art	48
Johnson, Bill "Tiger"	50, 82, 89, 131
Johnson, Charles	22, 96, 97, 154
Johnson, Jimmy	69, 96
Johnson, John Henry	21, 52, 132, 150
Johnson, Kilroy	8, 15, 22
Johnson, President	106
Johnson, Ronnie	8
Jones, David "Deacon"	124
Jones, Mike	38
Jones, William 'Dub'	92
Jorgensen, Sonny	154
Jorgensen, Walt	8, 61, 81, 89
Keefe, Gene	70, 93, 101, 106
Kelly, Gordon	58
Kelly, Rich	134
Kennedy, John F (JFK)	79
Kilmer, Billy	7, 63, 64, 68, 72, 75, 76, 85, 93, 98, 99, 102, 103, 108, 109, 111, 120, 121, 129, 139, 153, 158
Kilmer, Kathie	121, 122
Klein, Don	139
Klosterman, Don	144
Knap, Tony	90
Knibbe, Willard "Bill"	79
Kopay, Dave	64, 89
Kramer, Jerry	124

Kramer, Pete	31, 32, 99
Krowell, Adrianne	33
Krowell, Dave	8, 15, 22, 31, 33
Krueger, Charlie	7, 51, 54, 55, 57, 64, 82, 85, 87, 88, 89, 90, 91, 93, 96, 97, 99, 121, 128, 133, 154, 156, 157
Lagomarsino, Walt & Ernie	63
Lakes, Roland	87, 90, 97, 131
Lambeau, Curly	123
Lamonica, Daryle	60, 73
Landrift, Hobie	61
Landrum, Don	8, 29, 30, 99
Landry, Tom	53, 98
Lange, Paul	62
Larscheid, Jack	61
Lebaron, Eddie	53
Lee, Bruce	37
Levy, Butch	54
Lewis, Gary	88, 96
Lind, Mike	63, 64
Lipscomb, "Big Daddy"	56, 59
Lombardi, Jerry	8, 150
Lombardi, Vince	58, 85, 101, 125, 127
Lorenzo, Al &n Lynda	8, 26
Lum, Miss	32
Mackey, Dee	58
Mackey, John	151
Madden, John	127
Madrazo, Tony	60
Magac, Mike	58, 89
Mallory, Bob	23
Manning, Payton	119
Marchetti, Gino	56, 57, 82, 91, 124
Marin, Joe	134
Markstein, Al	134
Markstein, Bob and Laura	134

Markstein, Walt & Eve	134, 157
Marshall, Jim	85, 173
Massone, Bob & Kay	8
Mathewson, Christy	146
Mathias, Bob	52
Matson, Ollie	116
Mattson, Donny	20, 28
Mattson, Roy	20
Matuszak, John	141
Mazzei, Slats	8, 101
McCabe, Charlie	129,
McClay, Ollie	8, 15, 33
McDonald, Ralph	8, 139, 154, 161
McDonald, Ronald	122, 139
McDonalds, Ken	48
McElhenny, 'The King' Hugh	52, 59, 89, 92, 115, 132,
McGee, Max	65, 84, 142
McHan, Lamar	75
McInerney	90
McKean, Marv	8, 29, 35, 36, 37, 38
Mecom, John	111
Mellekas, John	7, 66, 121
Mendioil, Ray	8
Mendivil, Paul	8, 22
Menges, Gene	35
Mertens, Jerry	82
Milburn, Dr. Lloyd	94, 95, 96
Miller, Clark	87, 90, 92
Mira, George	85, 96
Monohan, Jim	112
Montana, Joe	127, 174
Moore, Archie	93
Moore, Lenny	69, 77, 78
Morabito, Tony	46, 47, 82, 115, 117, 128,
Morabito, Victor	129,
Morais, Mark & Linda	120

Mores, Cliff	28
Morken, Henry	61
Morrall, Earl	68, 119
Morze, Frank	56, 70
Mudd, Howard	7, 96, 98, 159
Musial, Stan	137
Myers, Jack 'Moose'	62
Myers, Joe	24
Namath, Joe	118, 119
Nevers, Ernie	92
Nitschke, Ray	87
Nolan, Dick	98
Nomellini, Leo	9, 51, 53, 54, 58, 59, 64, 75, 77, 78, 80, 81, 82, 89, 143, 150, 156, 162, 174
Noran, Carlene	8
Norton, Chico	79, 96, 108, 127
Norton, Jim	95
Norton, Ray	44
Nunes, Manuel	61
O'Brien, Dick	90
O'Neal, Jim	89
Otto, Jim	7, 46, 161, 167, 173
Owens, R. C.	7, 162, 173
Pachico, Don	31, 93, 191
Palmer, Arnold	83, 118
Palubicki, Grandfather Leo	18
Palubicki, Uncle Andy	18, 19, 20
Palubicki, Uncle Ernie	20, 21
Palubicki,, Grandma	18
Papetti, Sam	8, 165, 169
Parker, Jim	86
Parks, Dave	84, 88, 91, 96, 98, 102, 108
Parslow, Phil	7, 28, 29, 103
Pecciante, Leo	61
Perry, Gene	8
Perry, Joe 'The Jet'	46, 51, 52, 59

Peterson, Adrian	153
Pietrosante, Nick	56
Plumb, Ted	7, 11
Plunkett, Jim	27, 127, 128, 154
Pollard, Fritz	116
Powell, Gordie	15
Ralston, John	26, 27, 79
Rand, Ken	134
Rauch, John	60
Ravizza, Bert	62
Reagan, Ronald	106
Reece, Billie	4
Reece, Larry	8, 15, 22, 28, 61, 162
Rhode, Len	7, 50, 52
Ringo, Jim	124
Roberts, C. R.	58, 70
Robinson, Jackie	116
Romo, Eric	90
Rosenbaum, Art	144
Rozelle, Pete	79
Rubke, Karl	55, 91, 94, 95
Ruffo, Al	46
Salinger, Pierre	79
Sanders, Dick, M.D.	89, 94, 105
Sanderson, Doc	94
Sarris, George	60
Sayers, Gale	162, 173
Schmidt, Henry	70
Schwartz, Sid	106
Scott, Jim	105
Scotti, Ben	7, 87, 174
Scotti, Ben	7, 87, 174
Scotti, Tony	87
Serio, Mitch	110, 111, 112
Serrio, Jack	112
Shaw, Coach Lawrence T. 'Buck'	46, 47

Shofner, Jim	98
Shula, Don	127
Silver, Joe	106
Simmons, Lon	71, 89, 138, 139
Simpson, O.J.	128
Smith, J.D.	7, 59, 69, 72, 82, 88, 117, 121, 157, 159
Smith, Pam	99
Smith, Tom	134
Smith, Wiley	43
Snyder, Wilber	54
Soltau, Gordon (Gordie)	70, 71, 89, 92, 159
Sorrel, Allen E.	46
Spadia, Lou	49, 81, 82, 94, 98, 117, 126, 128, 129, 130, 143, 144, 161, 174
Spurrier, Steve	96, 98
St. Clair, Bob	7, 9, 10, 11, 52, 53, 56, 57, 59, 63, 64, 70, 75, 79, 80, 82, 89, 102, 116, 124, 130, 131, 132, 133, 137, 140, 143, 150, 157, 158, 162, 171
St. James, Margo	66
Stabler, Ken	127
Standridge, Bruce	134
Starr, Bart	65, 69, 127
Steele, Russell	8, 26, 28, 29
Steffen, Orval	30
Stickles, Monty	7, 56, 58, 64, 66, 78, 83, 88, 93, 96, 98, 102, 139, 157
Stonebreaker, Captain Steve	102
Strader, Norman "Red"	47
Strode, Woody	116
Stroer, Conrad	8, 12
Svihus, Bob	99
Sweigert, William	105
Szymanski, Mike	8, 101, 106, 137
Tarango, Pepi	90
Taylor, Jim	58, 59, 69, 73, 74, 84, 115, 124

Thomas, Joe	127, 128
Thomas, John	89, 96, 98
Thompson, Paul	8
Thorpe, Jim	146
Thurston, Fuzzy	173
Titchenal, Bob	36, 43, 70, 157
Tittle, Y.A.	7, 47, 52, 59, 67, 82, 89, 92, 96, 98, 118, 129, 132, 133, 139, 161, 173
Toler, Burl	116
Torres, Enrique	54
Touchstone, Don	134
Turre, E. J.	46
Uddleston, Jack	99
Unitas, Johnny	92, 118, 119, 120
Upshaw, Gene	154, 155
Varrichione, Frank	123
Venn, Mike	8, 140
Vera, Vince	134
Vermeil, Dick	37, 38
Villechaize, Herve	63, 64
Visentin, Gene	134
Voris, Dick	93, 97, 126
Vukad, Leroy	38
Waddell, Rube	146
Walker, Bob	103
Walsh, Bill	127, 128
Ward, Arch	46
Warfield, Paul	173
Washington, Kenny	116
Waters, Bob	56, 58, 88
Way, Fred	38
Wendryhoski, Joe	103
West, Bill	106
Wiggin, Paul	98
Willard, Ken	96, 97
Williams, Ted	137
Wilson, Billy	69, 70, 82, 89, 93, 98

Winkle, Walter	15
Wooden, John	120, 139
Woodson, Abe	7, 51, 76, 89, 143, 161, 162
Wrigley, Bill	123
Yankovic, Weird Al	87
Zubair, Joey (JZ)	4, Illustrations on 46, 164

Photographs and Illustrations

Mt. Diablo High School, Varsity Football, 1953	28
The CC Riders at San Quentin	41
Saturday Matinee, Christmas, Circa 1948-1950	24
My Year of Coaching, 1967	96
49er Team Picture, 1960	60
New Orleans Saints Team Picture, 1968	102
1981 49er "All Italian" Team	174